COVERED BY THE
BLOOD
of
JESUS

I AM COVERED BY THE
BLOOD—ARE YOU?

Rita Y. Jarrett

WESTBOW
PRESS®
A DIVISION OF THOMAS NELSON
& ZONDERVAN

Scripture taken from the King James Version of the Bible.

WestBow Press books may be ordered through booksellers or by contacting:

WestBow Press
A Division of Thomas Nelson & Zondervan
1663 Liberty Drive
Bloomington, IN 47403
www.westbowpress.com
1 (866) 928-1240

ISBN: 978-1-5127-0415-0 (sc)
ISBN: 978-1-5127-0417-4 (hc)
ISBN: 978-1-5127-0416-7 (e)

Print information available on the last page.

WestBow Press rev. date: 02/19/2016

CONTENTS

And they overcame him by the blood of the Lamb,
and by the word of their testimony.
— Revelation 12:11

DEDICATION

I dedicate this book of blood knowledge to my beautiful, gifted, third daughter, Rita Amia, one of the most profoundly talented writers God will ever create. Her sweet spirit hovers over these words and pages. I miss you, Ri.

SPECIAL ACKNOWLEDGMENTS

Special acknowledgment for contributions to this work go to Michelle N. Smithwick, MBA, whose loving and unselfish support, critique, and guidance kept me motivated and focused.

As well, without Cheryl L. Jackson's perfectionism, encouragement, love, computer mastery, and editing skills, I would not have completed this book and the accompanying study guide. These are the two wisest young women I have ever known, my "blood-covered daughters."

Thank you.

GIVING HONOR TO WHOM IT IS DUE
FINIS JENNINGS DAKE

Finis Jennings Dake's writings and revelatory comments have been a source of great help and inspiration as I wrote this book and the accompanying study guide, and it is necessary for me to give honor where it is due. I thought it most appropriate that I comment on this man and his anointing that pervades the pages of his annotated Bible, which has been a tremendous reference source and a source of enlightenment.

I researched his history and character and found he was indeed a student of the Word. According to L. Bible, Finis Jennings Dake was a twentieth-century Pentecostal/Charismatic theologian who was born in 1902 and died in 1987.

Dake was a theologian who had thousands of verses of Scripture in memory. Dake said he had received these Scriptures supernaturally at age eighteen in May 1920 at 2:00 in the morning while in prayer. In Dake's own words,

> Suddenly, and without warning there came
> over my being a cool and rushing wind. It

seemed I could hear the fluttering of the wings of a dove settling down upon my body. Then instantly, there came from the very depths of my innermost being the rivers of living water that Jesus promised in (John 7:37–39). Immediately I was aware of an ability I did not previously possess. I could now quote Scriptures, hundreds of them and that without any effort to memorize them. I just quoted as the Spirit gave utterance, and also I noticed a quickening of the Spirit in my mind to know and tell what chapters and books, various verses were found in. Thus Dake's ability was a gift from God. The notes in his Bibles show that he had great command of the Scriptures. There are over 500,000 cross references contained therein: more than any other reference Bible in the world. (Bible 1998)

Bible continues that Dake's "hermeneutical philosophy" was to take the words of the Bible literally when at all possible. If this was not possible in certain passages, one was to determine the literal meaning conveyed by the symbolic words. His belief was that God was perfectly capable of communicating with humans in a language they understood.

He authored several books. His most recognized achievement, though, is undoubtedly *Dake's Annotated Bible*;

he spent six years to compile his lifetime of Bible notes. Nationally recognized Christian speakers proclaim that the Dake Bible was the greatest Bible ever compiled. His knowledge of exact quotations of Scripture earned him the title "The Walking Bible" (2006).

I sincerely appreciate the dedication and devotion Dake demonstrated in his renowned and distinguished work. His thoughtful, profound, and revelatory commentaries have inspired and edified me. He has left a rich legacy that has impacted me immensely.

PREFACE

I became interested in and began this study of the precious blood of Jesus after hearing my spiritual Father, an anointed man of God teach and minster on this subject at various times during the thirty-two years I have been under his spiritual mentorship. I have since found that teaching and preaching about the blood as a vitally important and crucial lesson has somewhat diminished. My search for information led me to many bookstores, libraries, and other places to find information on the precious blood of Jesus. I became an addict; my search was relentless. Still, I could not find the answers to all my questions. I began to seek the Lord about this seeming lack of information on a subject so essential for believers.

I felt in my heart a pressing need to research and assimilate a book series that included a study guide and workbook integrator about the revelation of the blood sacrifice of Jesus Christ. This has become a lifelong mission for me, and since November 1995, when I began this effort, the more I got into the subject of the blood, the more it got into me. I was desperate for more on the subject but was frustrated when

I requested book catalogs from ministries and Christian publishing houses but learned there just was not enough in print on this subject, one that starts in Genesis and goes to Revelation.

My earnest attempt in this book was to provide answers to many questions I and possibly other believers have. I have tried to keep the information, truths, and revelations I have written more factual than simply supported with personal accounts. After a time, however, I began to realize how relevant some of my personal accounts were to my message.

I pray that all readers will develop an insatiable hunger for more revelation and knowledge of Jesus' blood sacrifice and for the most intimate relationship they can have, an individual relationship with Jesus Christ. They too will progress deeper into the blood, and as they become more involved, more power of the blood will manifest in their lives, to the glory of God. My intention was to write this book so others would learn how the Jesus' blood sacrifice affects them. "In him we live, move and have our being" (Acts 17:28).

My mission is to make much of the blood by any means possible and if necessary to create the means. I will offer some information to answer the first question, why did God choose blood. I will present some technical information to give readers a better understanding of what blood is how it works in our bodies, and its biblical significance. Scientists and academicians would not know the technical and scientific information I will present had God not revealed it to them.

I am aware of the appropriate syntax for nouns. However, in this book any name or word that refers to satan is intentionally written in lower case.

CHAPTER 1

WHY DID GOD CHOOSE BLOOD?

> For the life of the flesh in the blood: and I have
> given it to you upon the altar to make atonement
> for your souls: for it *is* the blood that maketh an
> atonement for the soul ... For it is the life of all
> flesh; the blood of it is for the life thereof.
>
> —Leviticus 17:11, 14.

We have redemption for our sins because of Christ's vicarious sacrifice and obedience to God. Eternal life would have ended in the garden at the foot of the Tree of the Knowledge of Good and Evil as the direct result of the sin of one man. Adam's sin of disobedience, a bite from the famed "apple;" it was the incident that shook the world's foundation. At that defining moment, satan became the god of this world; he unleashed on it every evil of his demonic imagination, a direct hit from the pit of hell. Earth became odiously and satanically corrupted from that one instance of disobedience. The father and author of sin, satan, became the ruling authority in the Earth.

Adam's sin was not unlike that embedded in the "I will" statements of satan. Isaiah 14:12–14 testifies,

> How art thou fallen from heaven, O Lucifer, son of the morning! how art thou cut down to the ground, which didst weaken the nations! For thou hast said in thine heart, *I will* ascend into heaven, *I will* exalt my throne above the stars of God: *I will* sit also upon the mount of the congregation, in the sides of the north: *I will* ascend above the heights of the clouds; *I will* be like the most High. (Emphasis added)

The operative words are "I will." Adam understood the instruction of God, as Genesis 2:16–17 testifies.

> And the LORD God commanded the man, saying, Of every tree of the garden thou mayest freely eat; But of the tree of the knowledge of good and evil, thou shalt not eat of it: for in the day that thou eatest thereof thou shalt surely die.

Webster's *American Dictionary of the English Language* provides the following definition for *command*: "to bid; to order; to direct; to charge; implying authority, and power to control, and to require obedience" (Webster, n.d.).

The Bible does not say Adam questioned God on this statement; he understood it. Adam of his own free will decided to disobey God. His "I will" was listening to the woman satan was using as an instrument of destruction.

> Free will is the freedom of decision or of choice between alternatives; the freedom of the will to choose a course of actions without external coercion, but in accordance with the ideals or moral outlook of the individual; free will is a doctrine. (Guralnik 1984)

In the beginning, God permitted Adam to eat freely from the Tree of (eternal) Life because God had created him to live eternally with him, as we read in our Scripture witness, Genesis 2:16–17. Adam had walked daily with God in the cool of the garden; such fellowship allowed God to explain to Adam what was good or evil.

God exiled Adam from the garden because he had committed sins of disobedience; God could no longer allow him to enjoy the fruit, eternal life, from the Tree of Life or Adam would have lived forever in his fallen state. God placed cherubim, spiritual guardians, with flaming swords to prevent Adam any further access to the tree.

The Tree of Life had a divine purpose; blood is a type of Tree of Life. A tree's trunk, branches, leaves, and roots are similar to the body's circulatory system; the arteries represent the trunk, the veins the branches, the capillaries the leaves, and bone marrow is similar to the roots. One scholar noted,

"The Hebrew language expresses the similarities between man and the tree by using the same terminology for both human beings and trees: *tsmixa*—growth, *Hipatxut*—development, *prixa*—bloom, and *kimila*—withering" (Choen-Regev, n.d.).

The word *blood* is mentioned "in the New Testament writings nearly three times as often as 'the cross of Christ' and five times as often as 'the death of Christ'" (Stibbs 1947). Blood is intrinsic to life. *Intrinsic* means "belonging to the real nature of a thing; not dependent on external circumstances; or essential or inherent" (Guralnik, 1982). The Tree of Life is intrinsic both to natural life and to supernatural, eternal life. In Leviticus 17:11, 14, we read, "For the life of the flesh is in the blood ... it is for the life thereof." Blood is not life; blood will die without the life force of God. The life force of God gives the blood life, and meaning.

God ordained the difference between life and blood: life sustains itself without blood, but blood cannot sustain itself without God's force of life that belongs supremely and exclusively to God. Life is "I AM," a manifestation of God's omnipotence. Life is God's "Let there be" force that brought everything into a flourishing existence. Life continues forever, even after the body dies. At physical death, life returns to God.

The force of life, meaning the "breath" or "spirit of life" belongs exclusively to God. "The word spirit is translated from the Hebrew word *ruach* and the Greek word *pneuma*, which can be translated as wind, breath, or spirit" (Vine, Unger and White 1996). One may construe the force of life, spirit, or breath as the spirit of life that returns to God, from which it came and to whom it belongs, as he is the creator of life. In Genesis 1:27, we read, "So God created man in his own image, in the image of God created he him; male and female created he them." God placed the spirit of life in every living thing. According to Genesis 2:7, "And the LORD God formed man *of* the dust of the ground, and breathed into his nostrils the breath of life; and man became a living soul" and speaking spirit.

Why did God choose blood to be the sacred vessel of our bodies in which life would reside? To help us understand this, we need to establish that blood was God's idea. The Jewish community of Old Testament times firmly believed this. When God prepared the human body of Christ in the womb of the virgin, Mary, he divinely and eminently prepared his blood to be qualified as the blood sacrifice sufficient to redeem the world from all sin. Hebrews 10:5 reads, "...a body thou hast *prepared* me." (Emphasis added) Just as he formed the body of Adam, he prepared a body for Jesus with all the human parts, including blood.

The word *prepare* means to "make fit, adapt or qualify for a particular purpose, end, service or state by any means whatever; to make ready, or put in suitable order" (Webster, n.d.). Jesus was prepared by God for both His coming, and going. God *declared* him his Son. God created, formed, made, and prepared the Word to become flesh and blood before the foundation of the world (1 Peter 1:19–20)! God prepared the life force of Jesus to be in his blood just as in all others. Jesus had to become man to die as man in order to pay the price for man's sin. God prepared his body and blood, which did not come out of God physically, for God is a Spirit, and God does not need blood to exist. I AM is its own power and the life force of all existence. God is the self-existent one.

The Jewish people of Old Testament times, and even today, had a sacred, reverential, and ineffable awe and respect for blood, they followed strict dietary, health, and sanitary laws based on Leviticus 17:11.

According to Steinburg (2003), "The Hebrew term for blood is *dam* probably derived from the Hebrew *adom* meaning red, which is the color of blood." In the Talmudic writings, the word *blood* was used to denote the essence of life.

> The Talmudic sages differentiated between various types of blood, blood gushing, blood flowing away, or oozing. The blood which oozes out after death and the blood of organs

that being the blood, which is within the organ, such as the blood of the heart within the heart muscle, the blood of the liver, the blood within the spleen and the like.

Steinburg provides a couple of specific laws as follows.

Specific Laws

Blood that flows from a live person even close to death but stops flowing when the soul departs does not require burial by rabbinic law. Dust near patients that contains some of the patients' blood is buried with them. If blood is on the clothing or shoes of a killed Jew, they are buried with that person lest some lifeblood be there (2003).

Steinburg stated that blood that oozed out after death is not blood that requires burial by rabbinic law (2003). He wrote, "It is forbidden by law to draw blood on the Sabbath for laboratory examination on the Sabbath neither by finger-stick nor from a vein or an artery. It is permissible only for a patient with a serious illness in whom there may be a question of danger of death" (Steinburg 2003). These laws come for the Talmud, a record of rabbinic discussions pertaining to Jewish laws, ethics, customs, and history (Steinburg 2003). Refer to the items listed below for further study or review.

1. Genesis 37:22; Leviticus 25:55; Deuteronomy 19:10; 2 Samuel 16:8, 2 Kings 21:16

2. Exodus 22:1
3. Sanhedrin 66a (see Rashi), Exodus 21:17
4. Genesis 49:11, Deuteronomy 32:14
5. Pesachem 25b, Mishah, Sanhedrin 4:5

There are explicit instructions regarding the elimination of blood from food (Steinburg 2003). The Jews had another reason for abstaining from blood as indicated in Leviticus 17:11, in which God said, "I have given [the blood] to you upon the altar to make atonement for your soul." "God, in his mercy, ordained that blood should be a means of atonement; for this reason, it is placed upon the altar, and man shall not taste of it" (Steinburg 2003).

The word atonement in the Bible comes from Hebrew root kaphar, which means make reconciliation, to cover over, pacify, propitiate by legal rites, and expiate (Old Testament Hebrew Lexicon 2013). It also means "satisfaction or reparation made by giving an equivalent for an injustice, or by doing or suffering, which is received in sanctification for an offense or injury" (Webster, n.d.). It means to make amends for a wrong or injury; to make good Adam's free will decision to disobey God. "The word atonement is used 80 times in the Old Testament and only once in the New Testament" (Dake 1996).

Jewish people also believed that blood that flows after a person dies is considered lifeblood that makes atonement (Steinburg 2003). It is the trading of that which lives, for that which brings death (sin) (Steinburg 2003).

It wasn't just the blood, but the life in the blood that made blood the acceptable sacrifice. They believed that this flow of blood must be collected and have it buried with the body, if there is too much lifeblood to be collected a person must collect a quarter-log, which is equivalent to one and half eggs, which is equal to a glass of wine! (Steinburg 2003)

How blood is respected, treated, and handled remains supremely important to the Jewish people, who view blood as the seat of life or the soul. All life originates in the breath of God; Psalm 104:29–30 tells us, "Thou takest away their breath, they die ... thou sendest forth thy spirit, they are created." It is easy to understand how blood became an object of sacred awe. It is, of course, not difficult to explain the origin of the prohibition against consuming the blood of beasts or birds or eating whatever is still full of blood. This prohibition was repeatedly, and explicitly emphasized in the Old Testament; this law was strictly observed, and its transgression was regarded as a grave sin.

Leviticus 17:11 tells us, "For the life of the flesh is in the blood: and I have given it to you upon the altar to make an atonement for your souls: for it is the blood that maketh an atonement for the soul." Jesus, of Jewish descent, held the same regard for blood, which He probably taught and preached. Blood is not just a physical entity; it is holy and sacred. Blood and lifeblood were things of reverence and remain so today. Blood is not simply a random act of God; it was his plan before the foundation of the world. Just as we are not of the world but in it, the blood is not of the body but in it to hold life. Anoint means "to consecrate by unction, or the use of oil" (Webster, n.d.). Anointing can also mean to be in the presence of God. It reflects the initiation of a divine influence, a holy emanation, spirit. Blood is holy in that it contains the life force of God. In 1 Corinthians 11:25, Jesus said, "This cup is the New Testament in my blood; this do ye, as oft as ye drink it, in remembrance of me." This is the "cup" of Jesus' blood, which gives life eternal, the blood that sustains itself by life, and the blood of atonement poured out for your sins. The word *blood* is used 329 times in the Old Testament and 101 times in the New Testament (Dake 1996).

We are guilty of taking the subject of blood too lightly. The life force defines the blood of Jesus; life and blood are synonymous; they are inextricable. Life is the "be" as in "let there be" force of God's, powered by his word. It was God's words "let there be", which brought even existence into existence. John 1:1 testifies, "In the beginning was the Word, and the Word was with God, and the Word was God." Life is God as God is **I AM.** Blood is an essence of life.

The Bible does not explicitly state why God choose blood; however, some Scripture provides insight. Leviticus 17:11 and 14 tell us, "For the life of the flesh in the blood ... For it is the life of all flesh; the blood of it is for the life thereof."

The *Old Testament Hebrew Lexicon* translates *chayah* as to have life, remain alive, sustain life, live prosperously, live forever, be quickened, and to be restored to life or health ("chayah," 2013). Genesis 2:7 tells us, "And the LORD God formed man of the dust of the ground, and breathed into his nostrils the breath of life; and man became a living soul [a speaking spirit]." This implies two parts in this creative act; God formed humanity out of dust and breathed life into humanity. This holy, oxygenated breath put the force of life in humanity's blood.

God knew how he was going to create humanity when he said, "Let us make man in our image, after our likeness [as a spiritual being]" (Genesis 1:26). Clearly, God made man a spirit first. Genesis 2:7 is when God formed man with a body, and organs, including blood. There is a difference between the words *created*, *formed*, and *made*. This leads us to consider further the thoughts of God. *Create* means "to produce; to bring into being from nothing; or to cause to exist" (Webster, n.d.). Genesis 1:27 testifies that before God formed man, he created him out of his omniscience, his intellect. Genesis 2:7 testifies, "And the Lord God formed man of the dust of the ground." *Form* means "to shape or mold. Matter is synonymous with the word *form*. Matter is "the basis or substratum of bodies; form is the particular disposition of matter in each body which distinguishes its appearance from that of every other body" (Webster, n.d.). *To make* means "to form out of materials; to fashion; to mold into shape; to cause to exist in a different form or as a distinct thing" (Webster, n.d.). Form also denotes "a gradual process in the work with great accuracy, detail and exactness." According to Genesis 2:22–23, God made Eve from a rib that He removed from Adams body. A rabbinic Midrash reported that Eve was taken from the thirteenth rib of Adam's right side ("Eve," 2011). This discourse finishes with Genesis 2:4–5.

> These *are* the generations of the heavens and of the earth when they were **created**, in the day that the Lord God made the earth and the heavens, And every plant of the field **before** it was in the earth, every herb of the field before it grew (Emphasis added).

This substantially verifies that God created all things. He is the Supreme Being, the first cause, the greatest self-constituted architect of the heavens and earth. "His workmanship exceeded the material or matter," derived from *materiam superabat opus*—Ovid (*Latin Dictionary*, 2008). What an awesome God we worship!

However, the blood, the body, and the soul had no life until God breathed into Adam's nostrils—the external beginning of the entire respiratory system, exactly the way it was designed by God! Our blood came alive by the Spirit of God, and man became a living soul, a speaking spirit.

Our blood is a substance from God that returns us to God by the blood of Jesus. Job 33:4 testifies, "The spirit of God hath made me and the breath [Nishma] of the almighty giveth me life." Since we usually associate blood with unpleasantness, why did God choose blood for his life force to reside in? Seeking an answer to this resulted in my writing this book.

I will briefly review scientific data regarding hematology, the study of blood. This technical discourse will help to provide readers with an understanding of God's choice of blood.

Blood is a specialized connective tissue that supplies organs with oxygen, which all tissue and cells must have to survive. According to Luckmann and Sorensen,

> connective tissue cells are those that bind together and support other cells and tissues. They include blood cells and skeletal cells. Blood cells carry oxygen to the tissue and carry carbon dioxide and waste from the tissue. (1974)

Oxygen cannot sustain life without blood to transport it through the body. Blood absorbs oxygen, having the ability to dissolve it or combine with it, and it does so only in the lungs ("The Human Body," n.d.). Blood, which is heavier than water, flows more slowly than water.

> The two fundamental properties of a fluid are its *density* and its *viscosity*. The density

is the mass per unit volume and blood is slightly denser than water. The viscosity is the resistance of the fluid to being moved. Blood is nearly four times more viscid than water. (Dodd 2001)

It constitutes about 7% of our total body weight. The blood volume is 10–12 pints of in an average adult of average weight. There are about one million red cells in 2 to 3 drops of blood. Blood is mostly water. The plasma part of blood is 90% water and constitutes 55% of the blood volume. (Blood Facts 2007)

The liquid part of blood greatly resembles seawater, and it contains salt, sodium, potassium, calcium and other minerals. (Eby, n.d.)

Blood's red cells carry oxygen; oxygen is essential to the life property of blood as it ignites blood to function in the body; blood cells cannot live without it. Blood carries proteins, a necessary food substance, to all parts of the body. The red cells carry hemoglobin, a substance that contains iron and attracts oxygen. The white blood cells fight off infection. (American Society of Hematology 2013). White cell also carry genetic material.

God exhaled into man's nostrils the breath of life, carrying oxygen via the respiratory and circulatory systems into the blood, quickening it with his spirit life.

Blood, a connective tissue, is a peculiar intimate bodily structure critical to the functioning of pulmonary circulation, which carries oxygenized blood from the right half of the heart, through the lungs, and back to the left half of the heart. The resulting cardiac output (of oxygen) must pass thru the pharynx, trachea or windpipe, then the lungs. The lung's air sacs are surrounded by blood vessels with very thin walls that allow oxygen to get through and into the blood; the blood then carries (life) and oxygen to every part of the body (DiGiovanna 1994).

All tissue must have an adequate supply of oxygen the first oxygen being the breath of God . God fixed this blood thing so that no one could deny He is the creator of life. It is a scientific fact that there is no substitute for blood and no indication there will be any in the near future or quite possibly ever. This is further proof that human blood is sanctified and belongs exclusively to God. Life feeds the blood life; blood feeds the body life (the life force of God). In his omniscience, God created our lungs with 600 million air cells to inhale 2,400 gallons of air a day and to function together with the circulatory system (*National Geographic* 2013). God breathed the breath of life into Adam's nostrils, the external part of the respiratory system that leads to the lungs. Both the respiratory and circulatory systems are orchestrated by God to function in sync with each other.

Psalm 139:14 tells us, "For I am fearfully and wonderfully made: marvellous are thy works."

Our divinely created circulatory system includes our heart, which "beats approximately 72 times per minute" forcing "blood into our circulatory system each time the heart contracts, resting only 0.4 tenths a second between each surge" (Luckmann and Sorensen 1974).

> [The circulatory system] has 970 miles of blood vessels, to work even while we are asleep. Circulating 2 ounces with each heartbeat, 4,200 ounces per hour, a tea cup every three beats, nearly 5 quarts a minute, 75 gallons per hour, 12 tons a day. Over 24 hours an average day it amounts to 70 barrels and in a lifetime of 70 years 18 million barrels of blood. In other words, enough blood circulates to fuel a car tank almost four times every hour just to keep the machinery of the body alive and functional at rest. (Luckmann and Sorensen 1974).

We can see that God has an architectural obsession for detail. God created Jesus' body with blood with the same detail He put into ours. Take a deep breath and feel your pulse in your wrist. Every pulsation represents God's life force; this is proof positive the life of the flesh is in the blood. This might also answer the question why God choose blood. Blood must have very special qualities that duplicate attributes of God's divinity, power, and glory. Could blood be a fountain of life?

Blood flowing through our bodies can be described as a smooth and uninterrupted movement of the indwelling Spirit of God. Our Scripture witness Jeremiah 2:13 tells us that God said, according to the prophet, "They have forsaken me, the fountain of living waters," and Psalm 36:9 testifies," For with thee [God] is the fountain of life." Vine, Unger, and White refer to a fountain "metaphorically, as the indwelling spirit of God" (1996). God placed in humanity a type of fountain of life, blood, with his breath of the Spirit of life. The blood's divine purpose is to hold life, begin life, and to provide a means for eternal life. In 1 Corinthians 3:16, we read, "Know ye not that you are the temple of God and that the Spirit of God dwelleth in you?" We were created to be a temple for God and within this temple is a fountain of life—blood. We are a sacred dwelling place of the fountain of life.

The two essential elements of our physical being are blood and flesh. Outwardly, we see and think of ourselves as bodies, but inwardly, spiritually, we are temples created by God in which he dwells and maintains a fountain of life—a replica of himself. This is now my spiritual definition of blood.

God provided blood as a type of Tree of Life, similar to the Tree of (eternal) Life that has been forbidden to us because of the sin of Adam. A type is a "pre-ordained representation wherein certain persons, events and institutions of the Old Testament stand for related and corresponding persons, events and institutions in the New Testament" (Dake 1996). Dake wrote, "Types are pictures or object lessons by which God has taught the people concerning His redemptive plan" (1996). "They are shadows of things to come and not the very image of those things. The Old Testament looks forward to the New Testament, the New Testament looks backward and testifies of the Old Testament" (1996).

A blood revival should break forth in our hearts and spirits to celebrate and acknowledge the price Jesus paid. *Revival* is defined as "restoration to vigor and activity; a bringing or coming back to life or consciousness; a stirring up of religious feelings" (Guralik 1982). Realizing that Jesus stayed on the cross until he took on himself all the sins of all humanity who were then alive and those yet to be born in to existence. The renewed knowledge of the blood sacrifice of Jesus will be a harbinger of the next revival.

Is the blood of Christ still alive in the earth? Our scripture witness 1 John 5:8 testifies, "And there are three that bear witness in earth, the Spirit, and the water, and the blood: and these three agree in one." Did Christ carry all his blood shed on the earth to the mercy seat, or does some essence of the blood remain alive and active in the earth? To provide some interesting insight,

> an expert in genetics, Dr. Eugene Dunkley indicated in order to perform a chromosome

count (karotype) test on human blood you must be able to isolate and culture living white blood cells. This is because white blood cells are the only cells in the blood that carry gene material. These cells must also be alive because they have to be cultured before they mature and divide. At a certain stage of cell division, the chromosomes within the cell become visible under a microscope. When this stage is reached a dye or chemical is added that stops the growth cycle, then the chromosomes are counted by sight through a microscope. (Fry 2003, November 11).

This is significant because further reading included comments regarding how this relates to the question, is the blood of Christ still alive in the earth? This article discussed how archaeologist Ron Wyatt

claimed to have found a sample of blood he believed to be dried blood of Christ which would be at least 2000 years old, which he stated when re-hydrated and examined under a microscope, contained living cells ... including white blood cells. The very fact that the blood of Christ was alive after two millennial this was considered nothing short of miraculous. (Fry 2003, November 11)

However, his statement is in line with scripture which speaks of Christ this way in our scripture witness, Psalms 16:10, "For thou wilt not leave my soul in hell; neither wilt thou suffer thine Holy One to see corruption." These are associated cross references of Luke 1:35, Acts 2:27, and Daniel 9:24. *Corruption* is defined as "the act of corrupting, or state of being corrupt or putrid; the destruction of the natural form of bodies, by the separation of the component parts, or by disorganization, in the process of putrefaction" (Webster's Revised Unabridged Dictionary n.d.).

The Bible provides a Scripture witness in Leviticus 17:11: "The life of the flesh is in the blood." We see that the true blood of Christ is as alive and a witness today as it was 2000 years ago. Our Scripture witness 1 John 5:8 reads, "And there are three that bear witness in earth, the Spirit, and the water, and the blood: and these three agree in one"; for the blood to be a witness in the earth, it would have to be alive. A witness is defined as "testimony; attestation of a fact or event; that which furnishes evidence or proof" (Webster n.d.). Whether or not Mr. Wyatt's story is true, we know there is enough divine power in the blood of Christ to keep it alive forever.

There is so much more to Christ's blood sacrifice than our finite minds can imagine. If we ever get a complete, in-depth understanding of the power of this beneficent, atoning act for our redemption, believers would become the most powerful "let there be" or "not be" force outside of the Word of God.

We must study to understand the value of the blood of Christ and the value that it owns in our lives. In 2 Timothy 2:15, we read, "Study to shew thyself approved unto God, a workman that needeth not to be ashamed, rightly dividing the word of truth." *Divide* means "to part, to open, or to cleave" (Webster n.d.). Vine's explains it this way: "handling rightly (the word of truth)" (Vine, Unger, and White 1996); we should not divide Scripture from Scripture but accurately understand it; that will keep us alive and faithful to God's promise of redemption and salvation.

Whenever we begin to appreciate, honor, and fully engage ourselves into the study of the precious blood of Christ, "There are three things that we may experience: (1) the immediate presence of the Holy Spirit; (2) an anointing of peace; and (3) the devil will send distractions, interruptions, disturbances, and outright attacks" (Hinn 1982). As John 10:10 tells us, "The thief cometh not but for to steal, and to kill, and to destroy."

The Holy Spirit is most closely associated with the blood of Christ. Where and when Christ's blood is acknowledged, the Holy Spirit will manifest himself as a comforter, teacher, truth, and power as explained by John 14:26 and 15:26.

From this brief discussion of the physiologic and scientific aspects of blood, it can be determined why God chose blood.

1. Blood is the exclusive property of God.
2. Leviticus 11:17 reads, "The life of the flesh is in blood."

3. Blood was designed by God to function in our bodies.
4. Blood holds life.
5. Blood has no substitute.
6. God prepared Jesus' body of flesh and blood to function like our own.

CHAPTER 2

THE BLESSING OF THE BLOOD SACRIFICE OF JESUS

And all these blessings shall come on thee, and overtake thee.

—Deuteronomy 27:2

The gift of God's only begotten Son and his blood sacrifice are the priceless gift for all of humankind. God is so loving and compassionate to humankind that he gave Christ as a willing sacrifice. We are blessed beyond measure by this, and we will never in this life understand this act of love. Even the angels were astounded by God's decision to do this for humankind. Hebrews 2:6 testifies, "What is man, that thou art mindful of him?"

In the synagogue at Capernaum, Jesus spoke of himself as the bread of life, his flesh and blood he would give for the life of the world. Four times over, he said most emphatically to drink his blood in John 6:53–56.

> Verily, verily, I say unto you, Except ye eat the flesh of the Son of man, and drink his blood, ye have no life in you. Whoso eateth my flesh, and drinketh my blood, hath eternal life; and I will raise him up at the last day. For my flesh is meat indeed, and my blood is drink indeed. He that eateth my flesh, and drinketh my blood, dwelleth in me, and I in him.

Our Lord thus declared the fundamental fact that he came to restore to us to our lost eternal life. Jesus could do this in no other way than by becoming a flesh-and-blood man and shedding his blood for us, thus making us partakers of its power. To "drink his blood" means to take into our heart, soul, and spirit the knowledge and memory of his blood sacrifice.

Grace and mercy are the arms of God's love stretched out for us as Christ's arms stretched out on the cross. He gave us the ultimate gift of eternal life, his blood. In 1 Corinthians 13:13, we read, "And now abideth faith, hope, charity, these three; but the greatest of these is charity;" *charity* means love.

The Blessing of Unconditional Love

Our first blessing of the blood sacrifice of Christ is the expressed, unconditional love of God. *Unconditional* means there were no conditions placed on the saving grace and self-sacrifice of Jesus; His blood is an expression of unconditional love. It does not fall under the "if we do or do not do something" condition whether we accept him as Savior or not. Jesus died for the sins of the world unconditionally period (John 1:29; Hebrew 10:9-10, 12; 1 John 2:2). All Jesus did to become human and die for us was unconditional love. The word *condition* means "anything required before the performance or completion of something else; provision; stipulation; pre-requisite" (Guralnik 1982). A condition usually follows the word *if*. God never said, "I will give my only begotten Son if …" In John 3:16, Jesus testified, "For God so loved the world that he gave his only begotten Son, that whosoever believeth in him should not perish, but have everlasting life." This passage contains not one *if*, and the word *whosoever* is significant because of its unconditional character or quality.

The love and blood of Jesus is our guarantee of eternal life and the proof and witness of God's love. We care about those we love; we are concerned with everything about their lives, but God knows the numbers of hairs on our heads and knows our thoughts before we even think them. There could not be this degree of interest if not for this degree of love. This great love God has for us is carried on and fulfilled in the blood of Jesus.

In 1 John 4, I found *love, loveth,* or *beloved* used 29 times, and they are found in the Bible 304 times. His love for us is holy; we are not able to duplicate it in any other relationship. Original love is God—the love of God, cannot be defined or described. We experience His love; or we can just take the Word for it. That is phenomenal!

The Blessing of Angels

Our Scripture witness Luke 1:35 testifies,

> And the angel answered and said unto her, The Holy Ghost shall come upon thee, and the power of the Highest shall overshadow thee: therefore also that **holy thing** which shall be born of thee shall be called the Son of God.

An angel announced to the Virgin Mary that she would conceive a **holy thing**. From the very day of our conception, the moment of our birth, throughout our lives, and to the pause (death) that takes us back to God, an angel specially selected, have been commanded to watch over us with the same intensity as with the announcement to Mary.

Angels bring blessings we should be mindful of; they are always active in our lives to save us from spiritual and carnal dangers; they help us through trying times. Hebrews 1:13–14 testifies, "But to which of the angels said he at any time, Sit on my right hand, until I make thine enemies thy footstool? Are they not all ministering spirits, sent forth to minister for them who shall be heirs of salvation?" The salvation we will inherit is eternal life.

The Blessing of the New Covenant

The new covenant is a blessing of the blood of Christ; Hebrews explains the new covenant in chapters 9, 10, and 11, in which Christ became man to shed his blood. This new covenant is the blood of God, meaning blood belonging to God. Jesus the Son of God made flesh is the mediator of the new testament or covenant (Hebrew 9:15 and Hebrew 12:24). He offered up his own blood, his life. God gave us a holy, spotless, pure, and eternal sacrifice for our sins. In the article "Tract 13f—The Crucifixion," Plutarch, a Greek historian of the first century, wrote, "Every kind of wickedness produces its own particular torment; just as every malefactor when he is brought forth to execution carries his own cross." Jesus paid the price for our wickedness and carried our cross to the cross. Because of our sin, his death was atrocious. It was our wickedness that produced the torment he suffered. We can own what Jesus did for us by appreciating his blood sacrifice and acknowledge his gift of love and great mercy.

The first covenant could provide only a covering. However, through Christ, we obtained a more excellent ministry established upon better promises. This new, better covenant bought with Christ's blood has redeemed us. The Old Testament was just a shadow of things to come and not the very image of those things; it dealt with the blood sacrifice of animals that could not leave a testament because animals could not be testators; they were dead sacrifices, and their sacrifice has ended. Christ is the only living sacrifice and testator.

A *testator* is "a man who makes and leaves a will or testament at death" (Webster, n.d.). While Christ had to die to put the testament in effect, he rose to ensure it was carried out to his exact specification. A testament is "a solemn authentic instrument in writing by which a person declares his will as to the disposal of his estate and effects after his death" (Webster, n.d.). A covenant is "a mutual agreement of two or more persons to do or to forebear some act or thing; a contract; stipulation" (Webster, n.d.). Although we can use these words interchangeably, they are different. Even though Jesus' sacrifice and animal sacrifice were blood covenants, only one became a testament. Covenants involved many high priests and many animal sacrifices, while the testament in Christ's blood involved one high priest, one sacrifice, once and for all for humankind.

The Blessing of the Holy Spirit

The Holy Spirit is also a blessing of the blood sacrifice of Christ, according to our Scripture witness John 14:16: "And I will pray the father and he will give you **another** Comforter; that he may abide with you forever." (Emphasis added) The characteristics of the Holy Spirit are holiness, peace, knowledge, truth, love, and power; they are gifts given to us because of Christ's sacrifice. We should thank God for giving us Christ in body and soul; we have truly been bought with a price! God held back nothing of Himself and nothing of the Godhead; he gave us his Son and the Holy Ghost.

The Holy Spirit is the "sanctifier"; Christ is the "sanctification." The Holy Spirit guides us to holiness and sanctification by demanding obedience, instant and complete. The Greek words *exousia* and *dunamis* translate respectively as "authority or privilege" and "power or force" (*Strong's Concordance*, n.d.). Our power to live holy to stand against the wiles of the devil and be successful in prayer comes from the blessings of the Holy Spirit. Both Greek translations for the word power are correct in explaining what these blessings of the Holy Spirit are for us. Acts 1:8 tells us, "But ye shall receive power, after that the Holy Ghost has come upon you." We received power and the gift of speaking in tongues from the Holy Spirit. Jesus had to die before the Holy Spirit could be sent as our comforter. This is a result of the precious blood of Christ.

We have the Holy Spirit's power to pray a prayer so powerful and intimate that the devil cannot understand or translate a single word. If the devil is left unguarded, he would wreak havoc in our lives, but he is totally frustrated when we pray in our heavenly language or speak in tongues. We have authority, power, and privilege beyond his comprehension. What the enemy does not understand is impossible for him to overcome or defeat. The devil has no defense!

We should worship God to the utmost. Our highest praise is not enough for His benevolent and supreme act of love, sacrificing his Son and sending his Holy Spirit. Everything holy and divine has been sent to us from the Father to save us and redeem us back to Him. We should never feel worthless; For with God we are worth everything even the blood of Jesus and the indwelling of the Holy Spirit. God sent his very best, his everything, so we would experience the fullness of the Godhead.

Our hearts and spirits should be overwhelmed with honor, awe, and reverence for the blood and all it represents in the Godhead. I am reminded of I Kings 8:11 when the priests fell on their faces and could not stand to minister because of the cloud—God's presence. Because of the blood, we walk on the holy ground of his sacrifice. We should not be able to stand and daily fall prostrate and worship like true worshippers. How can we be so stingy when it comes to giving God the worship he deserves?

We allow so many insignificant circumstances, people, places, and things to keep us from giving ourselves to unconditional worship. His unconditional love deserves unconditional worship. We allow ourselves to become more obedient and submissive to the circumstances than to our loving, forgiving Father, Creator, and Master. Only the creator of something has mastery of the thing he created. The wise sage who said, "Whomever or whatever you put first in your life is your God" understood that unconditional love deserves unconditional praise and worship.

No longer will we dare stand before God and offer pitiful, weak "hallelujahs" and "praise the Lords"; we must humble ourselves and praise him beyond what our stubborn, resistant flesh allows. We should praise the Lord as though his blood was always before our eyes. Jesus' death represents thousands upon multiplied thousands of times a death for all of us and also covers the unborn. He deserves the most prodigious sacrifice of praise. Until we do this, we have not given the honor that is his due, and we cannot enter the maximum fullness of all the blessings of the blood or New Testament in his name.

It is my most sincere prayer that the church will recognize what the blood of Christ represents. The blood sacrifice should not be a subject reserved only for certain times of the year but a celebration of the church on every occasion that the church doors open and throughout our daily lives. Where and when Jesus' blood is esteemed, the Holy Spirit will be present and will manifest his power.

The power of this acknowledgment could change the church forever. We would see the miracles of healing, prosperity, and deliverance we all desperately seek. Power would be the expected rather than the extraordinary, and revivals would be daily outpourings. If we have wondered when revivals will again sweep the land, we should begin anew to acknowledge the blood sacrifice of Christ for the power and purpose it owns and we will never be the same church.

The Holy Spirit is a gift; Luke 11:13 testifies, "How much more shall your heavenly Father give the Holy Spirit to them that ask him?" He comes to us on behalf of Christ's sacrifice to keep us from our "poison positions," the situations we are involved in that are contrary to the Word and plan of God for our lives. John 15:26–27 testifies,

> But when the Comforter is come, whom I will send unto you from the Father, even the Spirit of truth, which proceedeth from the Father, he shall testify of me: And ye also shall bear witness, because ye have been with me from the beginning.

These quiet but deadly "poison" positions can destroy our faith and relationship with God. We need a comforter, one who administers comfort and consolation; one who strengthens and supports our mind in distress or danger. American Dictionary of English Language Webster 1928 definition of the word comfort is excellent. It means "to strengthen the mind when depressed or enfeebled; to console; to give new vigor to the spirits; to cheer, or relieve from depression, or trouble" (Webster, n.d.)

The Holy Spirit administers comfort and consolation. He strengthens and supports us in distress or danger. When our minds are depressed, he relieves us of depression. I have heard many believers question, how can believers be depressed or suffer from depression when they know that God is immediately available to meet their needs? Depression is no different from any other sickness, disease, or illness; it is the illness of the soul, our mind, will and emotions. We are three-part beings. We have a soul, body, and a spirit all three can be attacked by the enemy of eternal life. We are saved from absolute destruction by the divine providence of God.

> The *Journal of the American Medical Association* in 1989 reported the clinical depression is the most incapacitating of all chronic conditions, in terms of social functioning. It ranks second only to advanced heart disease in exacting a physical toll, measured by days in the bed and body pain. "Major depression is far more disabling than many medical disorders, including chronic lung disease, arthritis and diabetes," says Frederick Goodwin, MD former director of the National Institute of Mental Health. Measured another way, the annual coast of depression in the United States was $43.7 billion in 1990, according to a study published in the Journal of Clinical Psychiatry. That sum represents a total of the cost of 290 million days lost to work, poor performance on the job, psychotherapeutic

care and the loss of lifetime earnings due to suicide. (Salmos 1995)

By the blood sacrifice of Jesus, we are victorious over depression. We should remember the crown of thorns that Jesus suffered.

> It was made from a small tree or shrub 10–15 feet high with plain white twigs. The crooked branches of this shrub are armed with thorns growing in pairs, a straight, tough, flexible spine and a curved one, commonly occurring together at each point. Its stipule has two vicious, long, sharp thorns, which re-curve backward, approximately 1–2 inches long. (Tract 13f—The Crucifixion, n.d.)

When the crown of thorns was crushed into the head of Jesus, it resulted in possibly severing several major blood vessels that feed the head, face, and neck. These thorny spikes would irritate, at the least, or penetrate the trigeminal lobes, and other facial veins, capillaries in the front and around the head and face including the occipital lobes in the back of the head causing an immense amount of blood loss and pain. (How He Died 2006)

Jesus' persecutors forced the thorns to penetrate even deeper when they hit him on the head with reeds. Shepherds used long reeds to control sheep. Jesus, the Lamb of God, suffered this torture as the Scripture witness Isaiah 53:7 testifies: "He was oppressed, and he was afflicted, yet he opened not his mouth; he is brought as a lamb before his Shearer's is dumb, so he openeth not his mouth." Jesus accepted the reeds beaten against his head in the role of a sheep. John 10:11 testifies, "I am the good shepherd: the good shepherd giveth his life for the sheep."

I believe the crown of thorns as it was crushed into Jesus' skull took power with each slash and puncture wound over every form of mental disease or disorder and every psychiatric anomaly. These are all covered by the blood, cast out, and halted by the Holy Spirit. Jesus is our great psychoanalyst. Therein is our cure!

Thank God for Jesus and his anointing, and thank Jesus for the Holy Ghost. He knew exactly what the believers would need after he ascended to his place and position at the Father's right hand. Nothing compares to the comfort of the Holy Spirit. In 2005, my precious mother went home to be with the Lord, and thirty days later, my youngest daughter was shot and killed by her boyfriend. I am a witness to the comfort of the Holy Spirit and can testify of his goodness. It is one thing to deal with the loss of a mother. For anyone who has ever dealt with the loss of child knows it is an entirely different kind of grief. We understand we may outlive our parents, but we never think we will outlive our children.

As any other parent would, I wanted to know what had happened. Did my daughter call out for me? Was she terrified? Did she suffer? I asked all the questions that come to mind when a loved one dies tragically. While I was making funeral arrangements and having quiet time with the Lord, I asked him to tell me what had happened. I asked if my daughter had cried out for me, and the Holy Spirit, the comforter responded quickly and comforted me with the answers I needed. He said very clearly, "No, she cried out to me. We had a conversation. She told me 'I love you,' and I told her 'I love you.' Then I asked her if she was ready to go, and she said yes, all this before the bullet entered her body, He went on to say, "I created time I can hold it still and turn it back if I so choose." In the space of time he held back, he talked with her and comforted her and even gave her the option to go with him or remain.

From that moment on, I was enveloped with a sense of peace I could not understand. My experience has been a comfort to others. I tell them about this intimate embrace of God's love and compassion for a mother who has lost her child; it lets them know God is **always** present in the life of believers, especially when tragedy strikes. I believe he gives believers an option with the question, "Are you ready to go?" Who could turn down a first-class trip to heaven in the presence of the Holy Spirit?

Because of the blood sacrifice of Jesus, the comforter was with me during the most trying, stressful period of my life. Without him, I never would have or could have made it in the word of the psalmist. Jesus knew we would have to deal with some heartbreaking and agonizing experiences but did not leave us comfortless. Believers can draw comfort from the work of the blood available to them and sanctioned by the Holy Spirit. The blood will never lose its power!

The Holy Spirit is comforter, teacher, leader, and guide who works directly on our hearts. We understand the Scriptures when the Holy Spirit reveals its (blood) meaning to us. The Holy Spirit makes the deep, secret things of Christ clear; he witnesses to our hearts, testifies about Jesus, and leads us to God. He understands our unique personalities, situations, and circumstances and makes the Word alive in us, at our point of need. However, He does require our willingness to be absolutely, obedient, and totally surrendered to the will of God.

Christ's blood sacrifice was not just for our redemption and salvation; yes, that would have been enough, but Jesus knew we would have to live, occupy, and endure in this world until his return. In Luke 19:13, Jesus gave a parable about this. Satan, the god of this world, would do all he could to make living, especially living Holy an unremitting struggle; it would be a nearly insurmountable task without the Holy Spirit.

Oh, The Blood, The Blood, thank God for The Blood! If Christ had not become a blood sacrifice, the Holy Spirit could not have been sent to comfort, teach and guide us. He teaches us to pray and to plead the blood according to the Word. Jude 20 testifies, "But ye, beloved building up yourselves on your most Holy faith praying in the Holy Ghost." We sometimes do not know how to pray as we should, but the Holy Spirit intercedes for us with groaning and leads us in prayer according to the will of God. Our Scripture witness Romans 8:26–27 testifies,

> Likewise the Spirit also helpeth our infirmities; for we know not what we should pray for as we ought; but the Spirit itself maketh intercession for us with groaning which cannot be uttered. And he that searcheth the hearts knoweth what is the mind of the Spirit, because he maketh intercession for the saints according to the will of God.

The Word became flesh. To fulfill the foreordained, Genesis promise to redeem, save, and sanctify humanity back to its perfect state before the fall. To accomplish this end, an acceptable sacrifice had to be made, and prepared, absolutely, sinless... Luke 1:31 testifies, "And, behold, thou shalt conceive in thy womb, and bring forth a son, and shalt call his name JESUS," and Luke 2:21 testifies, "His name was called JESUS, which was so named of the angels."

Fifteen Blessings of the Blood of Jesus (Dake 1996)

1. Atonement for the soul: Leviticus 17:11; Romans 3:24
2. Remission of sin: Matthew 26:28; Romans 3:24–25; Hebrews 9:22; Ephesians 1:7
3. Life and peace: Romans 2:10; Colossians 1:20
4. Redemption: Romans 3:24–25; Ephesians 1:7; Hebrews 9:12–15
5. Justification: Romans 5:9; Acts 13:38–39
6. Made nigh: Ephesians 2:13; Hebrews 10:19
7. Pure conscience: Hebrews 9:14
8. Cleansing from sin: 1 John 1:7
9. Sanctification: Hebrews 10:10–14, 13:20–21
10. New covenant: Matthew 26:28; Hebrews 12:24, 13:20
11. New birth: 1 Peter 1:18–23
12. Overcoming power: Revelation 12:11
13. Church membership: Acts 20:28
14. Salvation: Psalm 5; Hebrews 9:15
15. Salvation from an eternity in hell: Acts 2:24, 27, 31

CHAPTER 3

THE POWER OF PLEADING THE BLOOD OF JESUS

And they overcame him by the blood of the Lamb,
and by the word of their testimony.

—Revelation 12:11

A plea, an "urgent prayer or entreaty" (Webster, n.d.) can be a supplication for a divine intervention of God. When we as believers act on our belief, we can speak it to God in prayer without a doubt, and he will respond. The apostle Paul said, "We also believe and therefore speak" in 2 Corinthians 4:13. However, no magic formula activates the power of the blood; it is only by faith in Jesus' blood that power will be activated (Roman 3:22-25).

God supplied the blood so we could apply the blood. The water, which is the Holy Spirit, and the blood always act in concert with one another. Pleading the blood is an act of faith in the blood's power. When we truly recognize the need of in-depth knowledge about the workings of the power of the blood, it will be a life changing moment.

In the garden of Gethsemane at the Mount of Olives, Jesus pled the blood for us even while in the face of his crucifixion. Jesus suffered hematidrosis, a medical condition.

> Hematidrosis occurs when fear is piled on fear, when an agony of suffering laid upon an older suffering until the highly sensitized person can no longer sustain pain. At that moment, the person ordinarily loses consciousness. When the loss of consciousness does not happen, the subcutaneous capillaries sometimes dilate so broadly that when they come into contact with the sweat glands the little capillaries burst, the blood is exuded with the perspiration and usually, this occurs over the entire body. (Venes 2013)

Jesus did not lose consciousness, but he became so weakened that God sent angels to strengthen him. Jesus had witnessed crucifixions during his journeys. He knew what to expect Luke 22:42, 44 testifies,

> Saying, Father, if thou be willing, remove this cup from me; nevertheless not my will, but thine, be done ... And being in an agony he prayed [pleaded] more earnestly; and his

sweat was as it were great drops of blood falling down to the ground.

Hebrews 5:7 testifies this way: "Who in the days of his flesh, when he had offered up prayers and supplications with strong crying and tears unto him that was able to save him from death." Both passages speak of the agony of Jesus and of him pleading his own blood. We must recognize this example of Jesus and step across that border of our faith, which for some is just one small step. After slipping around it and peeking in from time to time, we finally surrender wholly to the blood's power. We will no longer be the people we once were. The blood is not something to be naïve about; we will become new creatures of power covered by the blood of Jesus. We must have faith in the blood demonstrated by our obedience to God's Word to plead the blood effectively. Without faith, it is impossible to please God, according to Hebrews 11:6. Without faith, it is impossible to believe in the power of pleading the blood.

Pleading the blood becomes an experience only for those who dare trust the Word made flesh by his Word and actions. There is no turning back because the blood has covered the way back. Pleading the blood is entering into another and higher dimension of faith I call "blood faith." Jesus' power on earth was also in his blood. Jesus was genuine in his sacrifice, and God was genuine in the acceptance of the sacrifice he prescribed, so we must be just as genuine in believing in the blood's power. It is the most powerful weapon we have against the enemy's assault. While trying to kill Jesus, he assassinated himself.

To plead the blood, we need an understanding of the power and character of the names and titles of Jesus; then we can apply that same power when pleading his blood. The name and the power are in the same, just as the Father, the Son and the Holy Spirit are the same. How do we apply the principle of pleading the blood to exact the power we need in a situation? We do this the same way we apply the principle of ministering salvation to lead others to accept Jesus as their personal Lord and Savior.

1. We must believe with our hearts the power of the blood.
2. We must confess this belief with our mouths.
3. We must believe in the power of the blood of Jesus shed for our sins.
4. We must believe that the blood of Jesus was accepted as he became the mercy seat at the right hand of the Father and will forever intercede for us.

Pleading the blood is spiritual warfare; it is the weapon of mass destruction and one of the weapons most feared by satan and his army. Every day of our lives, we born-again Christians are under constant attack by this adversary (John 16:33). The Bible tells us "be ye also ready" (Matthew 24:44). If we are always prepared, we do not have to get ready to face surprise attacks. We know we want certain things such as personal property, belongings, family, and loved ones protected at all times. Make it a confession of blood faith; I like to refer to as a blood-covered prayer.

Father,

In the name of Jesus and by the power of his blood sacrifice and resurrection, I plead the blood cover over my material estate. The power of the blood will destroy and circumvent any attack by satan or his evil disciples at the root. I plead the blood against demonic or human forces that try to come against me. I plead the blood of Jesus against any kind of disease, sickness, infirmity, or abnormality that would try to attack or enter into my body or those of my loved ones. I plead the blood of Jesus against any accident, natural disaster, or catastrophic event that may happen in my environment. I will be safe. Father, my confession of faith is that the blood of Jesus will protect me and prevent any successful attack by satan on my life or the lives of my loved ones, amen.

Individualize this prayer to fit your needs. Be specific, and make this prayer a lifestyle action and commitment. Plead the blood of Jesus before making any decision, especially before any travel. Pleading the blood is an offensive maneuver. Always be prompted and led by the Holy Spirit, the commander in chief; he will lead you triumphant in all your plans. Whenever the blood of Jesus is spoken, the Holy Spirit will manifest himself.

Believe without any doubt in the blood's power; Revelation 12:11 tells us, "They overcame him by **the blood** of the lamb and by the **word of their testimony**." (Emphasis added) Pleading the blood is the basis for the wording of your testimony, and overcoming is the result of your pleading. Once you know and confess this Scripture, you can let go into the blood all fears, doubts, frustrations, and anxieties. The blood carries an anointing inside and outside of our being. We will realize that by his blood we live and move and have our being (Acts 17:28).

We need to learn how to anchor ourselves in the blood. An anchor cannot be swayed by emotions, especially at times of tragedy when emotions try to overwhelm us and when we are likely to be caught off guard. An anchor is weighted to go deep and remain stationary, but an anchor in the blood is absolutely, unmovable, like a tree planted by the water. When we are anchored in the blood, our faith cannot be shaken.

The blood has a place in our soul—mind, will, and emotions. We must open our heart and spirits to the knowledge of the ability of the blood to protect and keep us safe.

I have become lost. No, not lost, but found in his blood; its precious power overwhelms me but keeps me safe. I look to God and our Lord Jesus Christ to give me balance so I can handle its power and prosper in its presence.

I have had to stop my writing this book to plead the blood to complete it. It has become one of the most important things of my life because I realize the magnitude of the assignment God gave me. I cannot quit even after all these years of research and believing and praying and waiting on God to inspire me on what to write and how to explain blood with deeper revelation and anointing. I wanted to hear from God how he wanted me to tell people about the precious blood sacrifice of Jesus. Only by the grace of God have I been able to do this. There have been many attacks and even attempts on my life during the writing of this blood, pleading the blood and anchoring me is how I persevered and maintained the victory.

Pleading the blood has made this book possible. I desperately wanted to make a difference; I am so much into the subject of the blood that it has become a big part of my life. I think, talk, preach, and teach about the blood to anyone who will listen. It has become my life devotion, my passion. Do not plead just innocent or guilty, plead the blood. The blood covers innocence and guilt. Plead the blood for victory over the enemy, for protection for yourself and your family, and for a closer relationship with God. Whenever you do, the Holy Spirit will manifest himself.

That is power multiplied that will insure your victory, and allow you to overcome!

This is an example of pleading the power of the blood to activate its inherent power. Just before Christmas 2007, my firstborn grandson was deployed to Iraq. Before he left we were able to spent some quality time together, and I had the opportunity to teach him about the love of God and the awesome power of Jesus' blood. I shared with him how it alone would keep him safe; this was my constant prayer for him and those who would be around him. He is a very strong-willed young man. In his last years of high school made up his mind that he wanted to join the Army. ROTC had been his passion and he loved it and was very successful. When we discussed this and the real possibility of his going into a war zone, he said "Grandma, we live in inner city Detroit. There's a chance every day, I could get shot or killed. At least in the army, I'd have a gun to shoot back." I marveled at his insight.

The power of the blood can be transferred by faith as it was with the "blood cover" my grandson used as a tourniquet. When I first started researching to write this book, I made red silk scarves for all in my family; I called them "blood covers"; they were to be carried or worn as a reminder that we are covered by the blood of Jesus. They became quite popular among my children's friends and many others.

I gave my blood cover, which held many prayers of faith over a ten-year period of my life, to my grandson to keep him safe in the war, or wherever he might go. I told him to remember the power of Jesus' blood. He said, "Grandma, I'll never take it off."

After his first tour of duty in Iraq, he told me that during a furious battle, a friend and fellow soldier sustained a very serious injury; his leg had been all but blown off. "Grandma," he said, "we tried the tourniquets we had with us. The first one broke, the second one broke, and even the third one broke. I remembered your scarf and used it on his leg to stop the bleeding. I always carried it with me concealed under my uniform. That scarf saved his life, and it has more blood on it now."

During another leave, my grandson shared other stories just as astounding as the first one. "Grandma," he said, "those people are very devious. They would think all kinds of ways to kill us. A woman would bring her three children with her every day to our campsite. She would plead with us to help her husband. One day, when I was not on duty, she came alone. This time, when the soldiers went out to talk to her, she blew herself up. She was a suicide bomber planning the whole time to kill us. I believe it was because of the blood cover that I was not there that day."

To plead the blood, you must believe in the power of the blood to conquer every situation. My grandson was only nineteen, an age when most young men believe they are invincible, and they are fearless. My grandson said he was never scared but always cautious. When you know you are covered by the blood, it is easy to be fearless. Thank God for the power of the blood to protect him.

Another incredible story he related was how the enemy saved pieces of reflective-type material from vehicle wrecks. They cut a shape of a dog out of cardboard and put the pieces of reflector as the eyes. They placed them in the road at night, which were extremely dark. When we were driving at night, it was hard to see clearly. Again, the blood protected my grandson; he was not in the convoy blown up by the fake dog trick. He told me of many dangerous times he and others had survived in the shadow of his blood cover. My grandson returned home without a scratch on him!

The mighty power of the blood of Jesus works. Who would ever have thought that that "blood cover" made ten years earlier would save lives thousands of miles away? God is good; the blood is powerful, and faith in it can be lifesaving.

Let the power of the blood have it free course. Everything it touches in your life will be precious and will prosper. The blood of Christ will take you every place you want to go and obtain for you every dream and hope. It will set you free to live life holy and free of drama. All the virtues, qualities, and characteristics of the blood will be available to you. Just as praise is to worship, so is worship to the blood.

The blood is a covering of anointing with power that knows no boundaries. There are no limits in the power of the blood. You will live it daily as a function of life like breathing. The blood is alive in you. It covers and envelopes. It is "love" blood. It is "joy" blood. Everything you need is in the blood.

Your lifestyle will plead the blood. Your ministry will be a blood ministry. You will live life as a result of coming in contact with the blood not just in day-to-day or hour-to-hour but in minute-to-minute intimacy with it. The blood will reveal and explain mysteries. It will become more alive to you. You will be covered by the blood, just as you are covered by your skin. It is a mark that you are sealed to Jesus. You will bear a living Passover door. More than a sprinkling, more than a touch on the hands, feet and head, the blood is your prayer answered, the deep calling unto deep. Be a slave to the blood and see your life change forever.

When you want peace, think on the blood of Jesus. How could it not have everything when it was before even the foundation of the world? As the Word upholds everything, so does the living blood of Jesus.

I have heard critics talk of the blood of Jesus as "slaughterhouse" religious thought. *Slaughtering* means killing violently. However, the blood of Jesus gives us eternal life. Those who refer to it as "slaughterhouse thought" have it wrong. We will live and not die because of the blood.

CHAPTER 4

WHAT IS THE BLOOD OF JESUS?

... to feed the church of God, which he hath
purchased with His own blood.

— Acts 20:28

Jesus' blood sacrifice will forever. It is eternal life. It holds the Godhead in fullness; it is the blood of God. Without this blood, there is no remission of sin; it is the ultimate power over sin, the substance of divine love and forgiveness. His blood is the strength of our life because in him we live, and move and have our being... It conquers all evil; it is the heartbeat of humanity, because without the vicarious blood sacrifice of Jesus humanity would have ceased to exist.

Our spirits crave for this anointing of life to bring us into holy communion with God. It is health and healing, the power of God manifested. To describe something so profound is beyond our capabilities; we can know it only by our spirit and the Word.

We have on average about 330 billion brain cells, and it is believed we use just 10 percent of them ("Your Amazing Wonderful Brain," n.d.). I passionately believe that the millions of brain cells scientist say we have that we do not use are meant for understanding the things of God. God created in us this huge number of brain cells to understand him and to praise him for who he is. Just ponder for a moment the level of worship and praise we could attain if we were able to use all of our brain cells for that purpose. The blood of Jesus is all that brainpower! The blood Jesus shed was a part of Jesus that protects us by its power.

God is indeed a force within us, and we should allow ourselves to be consumed by that force. Blood is a divine entity, a mystery of God's omniscience. An entity is defined as "a [holy] thing that has definite individual existence in reality or in the mind" (Guralnik 1982), anything real in itself. The blood of Jesus is not a person of the Godhead; it is a holy, divine thing belonging to the Son of God. Remember Luke 1:35: "Therefore also that **holy thing** which shall be born of thee shall be called the Son of God."

Thank God for the blood of Jesus! No words except perhaps the heavenly language of speaking in tongues can define what the blood is; that is why it is so vitally important we accept this gift, recognize it and use it in our prayer life. This will consecrate us to God in a way that dramatically transcends the limitations of our flesh.

The blood of Jesus is the self-evident consequence of God's great, everlasting, matchless, and sin-destroying love for us. The precious blood was foreordained before the world was created. Acts 20:28 testifies, "Feed the church of God, which he purchased with his own blood." Jesus' blood is the divine, precious blood of God. Yes, we know God as Spirit, but God created blood, so it belongs exclusively to him. Note that satan, a bloodless creature, is not able to have the God Spirit of life.

The Word of God tells us every male born from a woman's womb is holy; Luke 2:23 testifies, "As it is written in the law of the Lord, Every male that openeth the womb shall be called holy to the Lord." This is one reason why Jesus had to be born of a woman, not just created as Adam was. Blood holds life, and the blood of Christ held the life force of God the Father, The **I AM** power of God... The blood he sacrificed for us is sacred. We must be ever mindful that we never desecrate the blood of Jesus.

The Noah Webster 1828 dictionary defines desecrate this way: "to divert from a sacred purpose or appropriation; opposed to consecrate" (Webster n.d.). Jesus' blood was consecrated for the remission of our sins and thus is holy. Luke 1:35 testifies,

> And the angel answered and said unto her, The Holy Ghost shall come upon thee and the power of the Highest shall overshadow thee: therefore also that **holy thing** which shall be

born of thee shall born of thee shall be called
the **Son of God.**

Only holy blood could come from a holy thing. A holy
thing is sacred, and only sacred things can be desecrated;
desecration is a form of blasphemy, "an indignity offered
to God by words or writing; reproachful, contemptuous
or irreverent words uttered impiously against Jehovah"
(Webster n.d.). We must always honor and esteem the blood
sacrifice of Jesus with our words, hearts, and spirits. Jesus'
blood is the holiest substance God ever created because it
is the essence of God, it belongs supremely to him, and it
contains his power.

The blood of Jesus holds the power of *deliverance*, a
difficult word to accept; it is an old word that holds stigma.
If you are in a position from which you need deliverance,
remember the story of the man in Mark 5:5 who stripped
naked and cut himself. He was so far gone in his madness
that he did not realize he needed deliverance. But the
scripture says in verse 6 "When he saw Jesus afar off, he
ran and worshipped him," Some of us are so caught up in
circumstances that we are in a state of denial, indifference,
suffering, and mindlessness so deep that it takes more than
professional counseling (Christian or secular) to get to the
root cause of the issue. We need to be like this man run to
Jesus and worship Him.

The blood goes to the root and destroys it utterly. When
we are in a desperate place there is only one way out, we

must anchor ourselves in the blood of Jesus. We do not know what had driven the madman of Gadara to his mental state, but the only difference between him and those of us caught up in any addiction for example (which is madness) is that we have clothes to cover ourselves and are able to carry on a "front" of being civilized and in control. We need the power of Jesus' blood whether we realize it or not. We are totally dependent on Jesus. Every name and title that explains his character has a direct impact on how and who we are. Every name and title of Jesus is blood power and we should devote ourselves to knowing what each name and title means and represents.

Think about the Scriptures that say "in him" or "in whom"; this means we cannot do anything without him. Acts 17:28 testifies, "For in him we live, and move, and have our being." Deliver and deliverance means "to set free; to save from evil; danger, etc.; a freeing or being freed" (Guralik 1982). The blood of Jesus is deliverance, a first-line defense. Our Scripture witness 1 John 3:8 testifies, "For this purpose the Son of God was manifested, that he might destroy the works of the devil." Moreover, John 10:10 testifies, "The thief cometh not, but for to steal, and to kill, and to destroy: I am come that they might have life, and that they might have it more abundantly."

Our need for deliverance is separate from our emotional or psychological illnesses or diseases because we can also be delivered from bad habits such as smoking, overeating, and even nightmares, witchcraft, and fears. This also includes any situation that seem to overwhelm us. Freedom from evil and all its forms is in Jesus' blood.

One purpose of the blood of Jesus is deliverance related to the fact that one of the definitions of salvation is soundness and safety. Our part is to confess the Word in 2 Corinthians 10:4–5.

> For the weapons of our warfare are not carnal, but mighty through God to the pulling down of strong holds; Casting down imaginations, and every high thing that exalteth itself against the knowledge of God, and bringing into captivity every thought to the obedience of Christ.

Genesis 8:21 tells us, "for the imagination of man's heart is evil from his youth." We must believe Luke 1:37, which states nothing is impossible with God. Whatever may be the situation, circumstance, or simply put "that thing" that has so easily beset you and you have wrestled and struggled with possibly for years. It is a high thing that has exalted itself against the things of God. It seems that you just cannot shake it. The blood of Jesus is the key to victory. So what is the blood of Jesus? It is the burden removing, yoke destroying power of God (Isaiah 10:27).

Here is a special prayer for those in need of deliverance.

Father,

In the name of Jesus, I pray the prayer of deliverance. I plead the blood of Jesus with all the power of the Godhead to deliver me from the emotional pain of [_____]. I pray that the blood of Jesus will go to the root cause, pull it out, and leave no trace for it to return. I pray that the blood of Jesus disintegrate it and leave an anchor in the blood of Jesus. I praise and thank God I am right now free. No more shackles, no more chains. Your Word says in Isaiah 14:24, "The LORD of hosts hath sworn, saying, Surely as I have thought, so shall it come to pass; and as I have purposed, so shall it stand," amen.

CHAPTER 5

WHAT IS THE VALUE OF THE BLOOD OF JESUS?

In whom we have redemption through his blood, the
forgiveness of sins, according to the riches of his grace.

—Ephesians 1:7

The blood of Christ is cradled in and is the "I Am" life force of the Godhead, the only blood with atoning and redemptive properties. Romans 6:23 tells us, "For the wages of sin is death, but the gift of God is eternal life through Jesus Christ our Lord." Only the sinless, incorruptible blood of God can override the punishment of the law, as the wages of sin are death. The "blood of Christ" is mentioned in the writings of the New Testament nearly three times as often as the "cross of Christ" and five times as frequently as the "death of Christ" (Holmes 2013, April 19).

With the blood of Jesus, the law was fully satisfied, the Father glorified, and the future of mankind solidified. There is no remission of sin without blood. In *The Power of the Blood*, author Andrew Murray most eloquently wrote, "The value of the blood corresponds to the value of the life that is in it" (1993). Murray continued, "In the blood dwelt the soul of the holy Son of God. The eternal life of the godhead was carried in that blood" (1993). "Holy Son, holy body, holy blood!" Colossians 2:9 testifies, "For in him dwelleth all the fullness of the Godhead *bodily*." (Emphasis added)

We are not redeemed with corruptible things but with the precious, incorruptible blood of Christ. His blood was holy though he was born of the seed or through the womb of a woman to obtain legal entrance into this world. The blood of Jesus was completely pure and free of any contamination by sin. A review of maternal and fetal circulation indicates that the blood of a mother and her fetus never mix (Ziegel and Cranley 1978).

> It is now definitely known that the blood which flows in an unborn babies arteries and veins is not derived from the mother but is produced within the body of the foetus itself only after the introduction of the male sperm. An unfertilized ovum can never develop blood since the female egg does not by itself contain the elements essential for the production of this blood It is only after the male element has entered the ovum that blood can develop. (Remember Adams rib is

how Eve got her source for her continuous
blood supply.) (DeHaan 1943) Therefore,
Jesus obtained his blood from the Father God
(supernaturally).

The blood of Jesus was begotten of God; *begotten* is
defined as "to be born" (Vine, Unger, and White 1996); this
indicates that the Son of God was the sole representation of
the being and character of the one who sent him. God made
this plain in Hebrews 10:5: "Wherefore when he cometh
into the world, he saith, Sacrifice and offering thou wouldest
not, but a body hast thou prepared me." This body was
prepared holy with human characteristics. Our Scripture
witness Luke 1:35 testifies, "Therefore also that **Holy
thing** which will be born of thee shall be called The Son of
God." The blood of Christ is completely separated from sin,
evil and thereby consecrated and sacred, absolutely pure and
undefiled; the only blood type of its kind.

We are all grouped into blood types based on the work
of Carl Landsteiner in the early 1900s; we have either; A,
B, AB, or O blood.

Your Blood type is established before you
are born, by specific genes inherited from
your parents. You receive one gene from
your mother and one gene from your father;
these two combine to establish your Blood
type. These two inherited genes determine

your Blood type by making proteins called
agglutinogens exist on the surface of each red
Blood cell in your body. ("Blood Type Facts"
2013)

The blood of Christ, the Son of God, is the only blood that
is a "holy type," which was prepared and determined only
by his Father. Meditate and search the Scripture; did Jesus
receive any of Mary's DNA? Colossians 2:9 testifies, "For in
him dwelleth fulness of the Godhead bodily." Redemption of
the human race is found only in the divine power of Christ's
blood sacrifice. His blood is valuable beyond anything in
existence because of its supreme, paternal source. If not for
this, God's foreordained, divine intervention, we would
have cease to continue as the human race. In the garden of
Eden at the foot of the Tree of the Knowledge of Good and
Evil, the humans God created would have died and been lost
forever in the sin of disobedience and idolatry.

The blood is considered the seat of life (Leviticus 17:11).
Since life is the exclusive property and gift of God, it must
be returned to Him. This was accomplished as Jesus has
become the mercy seat for us.

Our Scripture witness testifies in Romans 6:16, "Know
ye not, that to whom ye yield yourselves servants to obey, his
servants ye are to whom ye obey; whether of sin unto death,
or of obedience unto righteousness?" When Eve yielded to the
serpent and Adam yielded to Eve, Adam became an obedient
servant—a form of idolatry. I believe there was more to

their sin than just disobedience. Obedience is "obeying or willing to obey; submissive; a giving in to the orders or instructions of one in authority or control" ("Obedience" 2014). Our Scripture witness 1 Samuel 15:22–23 testifies, "Behold, **to obey** is better than sacrifice, and **to hearken** than the fat of rams. For rebellion is as the sin of witchcraft, and stubbornness is as iniquity and idolatry." (Emphasis added) Romans 6:16 testifies, "Know ye not, that to whom ye yield yourselves servants to obey, his servants ye are to whom ye obey; whether of sin unto death, or of obedience unto righteousness?"

To take this a step further, *stubbornness* is "refusing to yield, obey or comply, resisting doggedly, or unreasonably" ("Stubbornness" 2013). Adam's idolatry could have been an excessive attachment for the woman God had given him, which bordered on adoration. The American Dictionary of English Noah Webster 1828 edition defines **idolatry** as "an excessive attachment or veneration for anything or that which borders on adoration" (Webster, n.d.). His excessive veneration changed his role of a husband from leading to following. Adam's sins were disobedience, rebellion, stubbornness, idolatry, and pride (Adam's will, not God's will). Witchcraft, in the American Dictionary of The English Language Noah Webster 1828, means "the practice of witches; sorcery; enchantments; **intercourse with the devil**" (Webster, n.d.). We could conclude that rebellion according to 1 Samuel 15:22-23 is intercourse with the devil.

Adam had been obedient in all things. Up until this time, Adam and God were alone together. We all know God said it was not good that man should be without a helpmeet.

God made a helpmeet from one of Adam's ribs. Genesis 2:20b–22 testifies,

> for Adam there was not found an helpmeet for him. And the Lord God caused a deep sleep to fall upon Adam, and he slept: and he took one of his ribs, and closed up the flesh instead thereof; And the rib, which the Lord God had taken from man, made he a woman, and brought her unto the man.

There was a blood reason for God's choice of the rib; ribs hold bone marrow, where blood cells are made ("Bone Marrow" 2014). This is why God declared that no bone of Jesus should be broken (John 19:33, 36).

We must understand that "adults have an average about 2.6 Kg or, 5.7 lbs. of bone marrow ... red marrow is found mainly in the flat bones like the breastbone, **ribs,** and vertebrae" (Dainty n.d.). The red blood cells are made in the bone marrow. Red cells pick up oxygen in the lungs and deposit carbon dioxide. In tissue, it reverses this process. After about 120 days, the blood cell is worn out, and it breaks down to give up its iron. This is taken back to the bone marrow and used to produce new red blood cells (OpenStax College 2013, June 19). There is no substitute for blood. God ordained that it be reproduced only in bone marrow.

"The awesomeness of God!"

Just think of his magnificent power that created our bone marrow to reproduce blood cells. It allows our blood to reproduce itself and hold life in our bodies. God's reason for taking a rib from Adam was to form the woman so that she would also have an unending source of blood supply like that given to Adam when God created him.

In Genesis 2:21–23, we read,

> And the LORD God caused a deep sleep to fall upon Adam, and he slept: and he took one of his ribs, and closed up the flesh instead thereof; And the rib, which the LORD God had taken from man, made he a woman, and brought her unto the man. And Adam said, This is now bone of my bones, and flesh of my flesh: she shall be called Woman, because she was taken out of Man.

Adam knew Eve had received his bone; he said, "bone of my bones." Adam had been in a deep sleep and would not have known this unless God had revealed it to him. Note that God did not breathe the breath of life into the woman as he had done with Adam; her life came from the life force of God through the bone marrow of Adam. This is important to remember later as we see the significance of bone and bone marrow in the life and body of Jesus.

God created for Adam this exquisite, perfectly formed woman. As Genesis 2:16–17 testifies,

> And the LORD God commanded the man, saying, Of every tree of the garden thou mayest freely eat: But of the tree of the knowledge of good and evil, thou shalt not eat of it: for in the day that thou eatest thereof thou shalt surely die.

Even though Adam knew exactly the commandment God had given him, he made a conscious, free-will decision to disobey God. Refusing to yield, obey or comply is a definition of stubbornness. It is important to note that the serpent did not speak to Adam. He was not tempted by the serpent, but by Eve to which the serpent spoke directly. Adam was totally influenced by her. This was not just a sin of disobedience but also of rebellion and idolatry. Even Adam admitted he had succumbed to the woman, not the serpent.

Genesis 3:12 testifies, "And the man said, The woman whom thou gavest to be with me, she gave me of the tree, and I did eat." Adam did not blame the serpent for his sin of disobedience, he blamed the woman. Adam's male hormones probably got the best of him and allowed the perfectly formed woman to overwhelm him. Even so, we cannot be too hard on Adam, as this scenario repeats itself with the men of God throughout the Bible and even today.

This event, however, was pivotal to setting the stage for the foreordained plan of God to provide an acceptable sacrifice to redeem man. The blood sacrifice of Jesus Christ the most puissant act of the Godhead because Jesus became flesh and blood. Philippians 2:7 testifies, "But he made himself of no reputation, and took on him the form of a servant, and was made in the likeness of men." John 1:1 reads, "In the beginning was the Word, and the Word was with God was and the Word was God." He possessed a perfect and complete human nature as well as a perfect and complete divine nature.

The union was *hypostatic*, "a theological term used with reference to the incarnation to express the revealed truth that in Christ one person subsists in two natures, the Divine and the human" (Pace 1910). In the incarnation of the Son, his human nature was united with the divine nature, but the two natures were distinct, whole, and unchanged; Jesus was truly God and truly man. His incarnation was more divinely powerful than his resurrection because if the Godhead could send him in the flesh, it could certainly resurrect him.

What also made the blood of Jesus acceptable was that as it flowed, it covered forever sin and death. Blood is not dead; it is holy. The word *holy* implies life. The blood of Jesus is alive because nothing about Jesus is dead. Life cannot be anything other than alive. I disagree with the idea that Jesus' blood is not physically alive but only symbolically alive. The power of the idea would have no effect; an idea does not have the power of salvation. His blood is alive because of the life force of God that existed in him.

What happens when the value of the blood is allowed to be perverted?

If we look back into history into the 1990's, we can begin to see a not so subtle perversion of the blood surface. We should understand by now that blood belongs to God. It is a creative vehicle or force to carry life. It is a holy substance by that standard. Remember when you study, let the Holy Spirit manifest himself. He always has fresh revelation knowledge just for you. Do not structure him out of your lesson. Do not lock the clock on Him. In the 1990s, the *Newsweek* online article referenced a summary of the American Religious Identification Survey by Jon Meacham. It revealed "that the number of Americans who claim no religious affiliation has nearly doubled since 1990, rising from 8 to 15 percent (Meacham, 2009, April 4). The author further shares that Post-Christian is an old term was revived with somewhat of a new urgency. It has meant different things at different times (Meacham, 2009, April 4). Meacham also states that a "more broader and for our purposes, most relevant definition is that "post-Christian" characterizes a period of time that follows the decline of the importance of Christianity in a region or society. This use of the phrase first appeared in the 1929 book "America Set Free" by German philosopher

Hermann Keyserin (April 4, 2009). The article went on to say "this is not to say that the Christian God is dead, but that he is less of a force in American politics and culture than at any other time in recent memory" (Meacham, 2009, April 4). "The term [post-Christian] was popularized during what scholars call the "death of God" movement of the mid 1960s— a movement that is, in its way, still in motion" (Meacham, 2009, April 4).

According to Meacham, "In 1992 the critic Harold Bloom published a book titled "The American Religion: The Emergence of the Post-Christian Nation." In it he cites William James's definition of religion in "The Varieties of Religious Experience." *"Religion... shall mean for us the feelings, acts, and experiences of individual men in their solitude, so far as they apprehend themselves to stand in relation to whatever they consider the divine""* (April 4, 2009).

"According to the American Religious Identification Survey, ...the percentage of self-identified Christians has fallen 10 percentage points since 1990, from 86 to 76 percent... A separate poll echoed the ARIS finding, reporting that that percentage of people who say they are unaffiliated with any particular faith has doubled in recent years, to 16 percent" (Meacham, 2009, April 4). "Two-thirds of the public (68 percent), now say religion is "losing its influence" in American society, while just 19 percent say religion's influence is on the rise. The proportion of Americans who think religion "can answer all or most of today's problems" is now as a historic low of 48 percent" (Meacham, 2009, April 4).

While these facts were coming to light, other cultural changes were taking place as well. Our scripture witness, Ephesians 4:27, testifies "Neither give place to the devil." Somehow a door was left wide open for him in the 1960s-1990s because this all just didn't happen overnight. We must remember, our scripture witnesses, Isaiah 14:14 and 2 Thessalonians 2:4, which testify respectively "I will ascend above the heights of the clouds; I will be like the most High." and pair that with "Who opposeth and exalteth himself above all that is called God..." We realize that this is satan's plan. "His I will" comments are meant to pervert everything that God is by thinking he (satan) can be like him. Blood belongs to God exclusively. The vampire culture that was introduced during this time is a demonic perversion of the blood.

Melton writes that we begin to see the vampire culture in comic books, such as Marvel in the 1970s version of Dracula and by the late 1970s on silver screen. Universal Films produced Dracula in1979 and at least 10 movies between 1979 and 1992. It seemed there was a lust for vampire movies (Melton, 1994). Especially with the capabilities of video recorder and cable TV, vampire movies had unlimited outlet and exposure. It was almost unprecedented more and more novels were being written as well as comic books and new characters being developed. Sixty percent of all vampire novels written have appeared in the last 30 years (Melton, 1994).

The question was raised; what was the underlying fascination with the vampire theme? Many guessed death, passion, horror, rebellion, mystery, immortality maybe, power.

The main characteristic shared by vampires, or this type of demonic spirits is their insatiable need for blood, which they drain from the bodies of God created living human beings.

During my research, I was shocked to discover how much of the vampire culture that we had allowed to slip by us. Even the children are being introduced to their own level of vampire entertainment. **Bunnicula** a children's book series was written by James Howe (and his late wife Deborah), in the case of "Bunnicula." it is about a vampire bunny that sucks the juice out of vegetables. It is also the name of the first book series published in1979.

"A 1979 animated TV special (from Ruby-Spears) by the same name was created based on the first book and aired on the ABC Weekend Special. The animated special deviated heavily from the novels and actively depicted Bunnicula using vampiric powers, which did not occur in the novels" (Melton, 1994). "Count Duckcula a series first aired in the USA in 1989-1993 on Nickelodeon. The story is that Duckcula has been active as vampire for centuries but was accidentally given tomato ketchup instead of blood so he is not a blood-sucking vampire, but a vegetarian one. However, all of his relatives are real vampires from all over the world" (Melton, 1994).

Melton inscribes that it was also around this same time the New Gothic Movement started, 1980 traced back to 1970's. Those enthralled by this new culture were also thought to be inspired by the vampire image. There are more than 650 movies or films about the subject of vampires or vampire themes. There were 573 books or novels, 63 of which have extreme titles with the word blood in them, for example, Blood Will Have Blood; In The Blood; Precious Blood; Those of My Blood; Life Blood; 57 plays. These are numbers of books just up until 1970. There are also about 32 Vampire Guilds or organizations in America (1984).

"During the time span of 1966 to 1971, The World of Dark Shadows was on ABC; later not to be out done in, 1991, NBC offered its audience the soap-opera: The World of Dark Shadows" (Melton, 1984).

Just what kind of power is behind all this? Notice the time line carefully. The Church of Satan is founded, April 30 1966 by Anton La Vey (Wikipedia, 2014). Later the Temple of Set is founded in 1972 by Michael Aquino supposedly, the successor to the Church of Satan (Wikipedia, 2014) **(NOTE: As this book is about Jesus' blood, it was not important for us to do an in depth research on this satanic related topic.)**

It is one to the churches primary responsibilities to protect the value, sacredness and holiness of the blood. Allowing any kind of perversion of it is sin. The Bible is very clear that blood belongs to God. Not only are we allowing ourselves to be subjected to demonic images of eating blood, but we have allowed a generation of children to witness the demonic spirit of vampires in books, films, etc. This is even a cereal called Count Chocula.

We hear our preachers say on Sunday morning, Lord have your way. However, the Holy Spirit also hears him say, but can you do it after my "Five keys to Happy Heaven" or "Ten Points to a Good Life." We are grieving the Holy Spirit. He sees the attack. He knows that the people may be seeing and hearing more about the blood from vampire movies and books than they are hearing in the church. My point being, where are the 650 movies about the Blood of Jesus? Where are our 30 new teaching books that are coming out each month about the Blood of Jesus? Where is our focus, church?

Did you notice the time line? The interest in Vampires peaked at the same time as the Church of Satan was founded 1966-1975. The Newsweek article noted the number of people with a disinterest or no church affiliation doubled by 1990 (Meacham, 2009, April 4). No, it was not all about vampire movies, but it was about a move toward perversions of the blood and away from God.

Remember satan is a liar. The Bible says he is the Father of lies (John 8:44). Satan is a demonic spirit. He has no **human body** or **blood that is why he wants to possess yours!**

The blood of Jesus Christ is what brought us salvation and redemption. It has released us forever from the power of the devil, and we once again have the promise eternal life with the Father, God. Our scripture witness, Hebrews 9:22, testifies "... without the shedding of blood there is no remission" [of sin]. It is because of what the blood of Jesus did for us that satan hates it. He wants to use every diabolical method to devalue it and pervert its spiritual meaning and power to the world.

It is up to us, to the church, to ensure that the value of the blood is protected. That is kept Holy and sanctified. That we increase our knowledge and teaching about the power of the blood of Jesus. That it is alive and that it is the churches responsibility to, as Jesus said, do this in remembrance of me. He has asked us to give value and honor to his body that was broken for us and to his blood that was given.

CHAPTER 6

HEALING POWER IN THE BLOOD OF JESUS

Who his own self bare our sins in his own body on the tree, that we being dead to sins, should live unto righteousness; by whose stripes ye were healed.

—1 Peter 2:24

The blood is the proof of the "I will" of Jesus. Mark 1:40–41 testifies,

> And there came a leper to him, beseeching him, and kneeling down to him, and saying unto him, **If thou will**, thou canst make me clean. And Jesus, moved with compassion, put forth his hand, and touched him, and saith unto him, **I will**; be thou clean.(Emphasis added)

"I will" is more than a promise; it is a *vow* and covenant between Father and Son for divine healing that can never be broken. Psalm 138:2 testifies, "For thou hast magnified thy word above thy name."

Jesus could heal while he was on earth because the power was in his blood, and it remains with us. Just as the Holy Spirit remains our comforter, Jesus prescribes and the Holy Spirit dispenses.

What a promise! This is a covenant promise so many of us are praying. We believe for our healing and believe that he can, but not that he will. The leper was healed because he knew Jesus could heal him. Like many of us, he was not sure Jesus was willing. Believing God can do what his Word says he can do is easy for us; however, we have a problem believing he will. Well, my dear sisters and brothers, here is something to shout about as Matthew 8:2–3 testifies,

> And, behold, there came a leper and worshiped him, saying, Lord, **if thou wilt**, thou canst make me clean. And Jesus put forth his hand, and touched him, saying, **I will;** be thou clean. And immediately his leprosy was cleansed. (Emphasis added)

"He is willing. Therefore, there should be no room for doubt. He can and he will.

He is willing, and we should not doubt he will. If for some demonic reason you are still wavering, read John 9:3–4: "Jesus answered, Neither hath this man sinned, nor his parents; but that the works of God should be made manifest in him. I must perform the works of him that sent me." Jesus was telling us that healing is a work of God; a work that God had sent him to perform. It is a work that was in his blood sacrifice for our salvation. *Salvation* also means "healing." Our Scripture witness 1 Peter 2:24 testifies, "Who his own self bare our sins in his own body on the tree, [cross] that we, being dead to sins, should live unto righteousness: by whose stripes ye were healed." One of satan's greatest triumphs is keeping us believing we are sick, cannot be healed, and are unworthy to receive God's healing, God provided, promised and guaranteed by Jesus' stripes. Our healing is written in blood!

I believe the devil has a special demonic task force just for this purpose; that is why we must lock into our faith so that the forces of hell cannot prevail against it. We must believe the Word of God that Jesus can, will, and has already healed us. The Word of God is full of passages on healing; find those that touch your heart that carry a special meaning to you and let them anoint your faith. You must believe, and he will perform.

Think about this. If the (virtue) power came out of Jesus when the woman with the issue of blood touched just the hem of his garment, his clothes, just imagine what kind of power or virtue comes out of his blood! According to Webster's 1828 dictionary, virtue means "acting power, something efficacious" (Webster, n.d.). Our Scripture witness Mark 5:30 testifies, "And Jesus, immediately knowing in himself that virtue [power] had gone out of him; turned him about in the press, and said, who touched my clothes?" Our second Scripture witness is even more compelling; Luke 6:19 testifies, "And the whole multitude sought to touch him: for there went virtue out of Him, and **healed them all**."(Emphasis added)

Are you praying the faith that you have in the blood and in the promises of the Word? Pray your faith. The enemy attacks our faith to kill us; this is one of the primary reasons for sickness and disease. We need to maintain an addictive obsession to receiving and keeping the power of healing in our lives; this is the secret to the divine, eternal healing we need.

The most influential power source to help us do this is the blood of Jesus. Jesus shed his own blood for our healing. He meant it to be the remedy, cure and eradicator of incipient death. Incipient death is exactly what sickness and disease are in our bodies.

Jesus killed the power of sickness, disease, and death with his body and blood, so sickness and disease do not have any power except what we allow by not acknowledging and confessing the blood cover provided by the blood sacrifice of Jesus. Healing is one of the divine reasons he came in the flesh.

I had my own personal opportunity to put this into practice in 2005. After I fell down some cement steps, I begin to have symptoms of chest pain. During my visit to the emergency room, the hospital performed a chest x-ray. The results of the x-ray revealed that there was a mass in the right side of my chest deep under my breastbone. I had no symptoms or any indication that there was anything wrong. The emergency room doctor asked if I wanted to have an MRI done or if I wanted to wait and see my personal physician. I consented to have the test done immediately and at that very same moment I felt the power and comfort of the Holy Spirit rise up in me, alert and ready. I actually felt a stirring in my spirit. I guess a better way to describe it would to be saying, I felt a move of the Holy Spirit within me.

A few days later, after I had seen my personal physician, the madness started. He referred me to a specialist. One day you are OK and the very next faced with a possible life and death situation. The specialist I saw told me the mass I had could be a precursor of a form of Cancer called a Thymoma. An incredible calmness enveloped me during this entire process. I knew immediately that it was the comfort of the Holy Spirit.

The fight was on. The Scripture that touched my heart and carried a special meaning and anointing for me was Matthew 9:28–29, which I paraphrase here: "'Do you, Rita, believe that I am able to do this?' 'Yes, Lord,' I replied. He touched me and said, 'According to your faith, it will be done to you.'"

I had my daughter type, and frame this Scripture so I could keep it by my bedside at the hospital to remind me of God's promise in his Word. It would also speak volumes for any visitors who did not know what to say. I did not want anything but the word *confessed* over me during this critical time. I offer the same advice to you. Make it clear to everyone what you believe and expect to come to pass. Never leave any room for doubt or conjecture. If you give the enemy an inch, he will take a mile. Always protect your healing. Keep only scriptural and positive confessions and people who believe them around you.

The Sunday before the surgery, I decided to praise God with all the spiritual passion I had. I was going to celebrate my victory until I was totally spent physically and spiritually. I danced, shouted, sang, and praised God until I fell under the power of the Holy Spirit. I believe that this is when the fullness of the blessing took place. That was nothing compared to the ultimate outcome. Because of Jesus' blood, we have a covenant with better promises and the best results.

After I got home from the hospital, I had to wait for over a week for the results of the biopsy. My children called me almost daily asking me what the results were; they thought I knew but was not telling them. What they did not understand was I knew that the blood of Jesus was stronger than any report.

The doctor finally called and said what I already knew in my spirit—the tumor was benign; I did not have cancer. I didn't know that my personal physician, an excellent doctor I must say, had been present during the surgery, but I remembered him being at my bedside and saying to me soon after my surgery, "We don't know what that 'black thing' was we pulled out of your chest, but you came through the surgery okay."

I knew what it was and after I got a copy of the biopsy results it proved the blood of Jesus power. They had removed a golf-ball sized mass of necrotic, or dead, tissue, from my chest. Well isn't that amazing, **necrotic tissue is dead tissue**. It was dead because I had prayed the power of the blood of Jesus to destroy the ungodly mass at the root. I am a living witness that he can heal, he will heal, he is healing, and he has healed. His name is "I Am, I Will." Some of us who maybe experiencing a seemly, "manifestation delay" should start calling Him "I Am, I Will." Just as Abraham's name change changed his mind-set, this can change yours. Call those the things which be not as though they were (Romans 4:17). Signs and symptoms no longer have any power. You should be saying, "I am healed."

Faith is your manifestation. The manifestation does not make healing a reality, his blood and Word do. His Word is your guarantee. Healing is in the "I will" of Jesus. Just believe it, and it is already done. Praise God for that. As a matter of "faith" fact, it is done whether it is ever manifested. Isaiah 55:11 testifies, "So shall my word be that goeth forth out of my mouth: it shall not return unto me void, but it shall accomplish that which I please, and it shall prosper in the thing whereto I sent it." And Psalm 119:89 testifies, "For ever O Lord, thy word, is settled in heaven"; this confirms the first. If what the Word says about healing is not true, it is all a lie. Close the book and die. I believe he will and can raise you up one way or another dead or alive.

Our Scripture witness Romans 8:11 testifies, "But the Spirit of him that raised up Jesus from the dead dwell in you, he that raised up Christ from the dead shall also quicken your mortal bodies by his Spirit that dwelleth in you." We might as well just believe the Word. Healing faith believes the Word of God, not the circumstances of signs and symptoms. The only evidence we need is the blood of Jesus. By his stripes we were and are healed. This is not scientific evidence; it is spiritual until physically manifested. Healing is a blood-kept promise.

I believe healing is always present immediately when we pray. Any time lapse of the manifestation is because our faith has to rise to the level of the healing power of God. It is when our faith meets the level of the healing power that healing is manifest. God is omnipresent with his word. We sometimes do not realize the immediate presence or manifestation because we are not spiritually conscience or aware of the anointing that is taking place in our bodies for any number of reasons.

God's Word is truth; anything else is a lie opposed to the Word. We must always be cognizant of the fact that just as the Word is opposed by the devil, so is our healing and wholeness. Just as he comes to take away the Word, he also comes to take away the manifestation of the Word, in this instance, healing. Remember he comes only to kill, steal, and destroy.

My dear sisters and brothers, believe God's word and promises of healing. It is the blood covenant of his life given for us to be whole, as in him we live and move and have our being. Our Scripture witness 1 Corinthians 11:25 testifies, "This cup is the new covenant in my blood; do this, whenever you drink it, in remembrance of me." Jesus was saying he is our healer who gave his life for ours. His love is so deep for us that he wants our wholeness to be an expression of his love.

Jesus loves us so much that it is difficult for him to determine where we leave off and he begins. Love requires intimacy, which requires wholeness. Those who are in faith for healing must be close to God. We must lose ourselves in his love in the power of his presence and in his Word. That is where we will find healing and appropriate it. It cannot be found without him; it is who he is.

The blood sacrifice of Jesus is the only medicine we need. I am not advocating giving up medication or treatment; what

I am saying is that he is the healing power we need. Honor his blood sacrifice, praise and worship Him, and believe and confess the Word. Remember the covenant of the blood sacrifice between the Father and his Son.

CHAPTER 7

THE BLOOD OF JESUS KEEPS US FROM HELL

I am he that liveth and was dead; and, behold, I am alive for evermore, Amen; and have the keys of hell and of death.

—Revelation 1:8

The Bible speaks of eternal life in heaven and hell. We received free will to choose our fate. God has done everything possible to keep us from an eternity in hell, but it is up to us to make the ultimate decision.

God in his sovereignty loved us so much that he even allowed us to choose to serve him or not. He did not create us automatons or robots but made us in his image. I prudently caution you, however, not to let free will send you to hell. Jesus suffered the most agonizing and cruel death of any man ever. His horrible death was necessary because the punishment had to fit the crime of our sin.

No one else could have taken on the sins of the whole world. When we realize this, we can begin to understand why the methods used to kill him were so barbaric and horrific. However, his death by crucifixion was only a glimpse of the torments of hell. Jesus became flesh to take our place; we do not have to go there. We do not have to suffer the horrors of hell as he did during his time there. After his victory over satan, he rose from hell with the keys of hell and death. He triumphed over satan and hell and he was the only one who has gone there, paid the price for sin, then able to leave by the power of the Godhead to return to Earth, and ascend to his right place in Heaven.

Hell is an eternal madness. It is the epitome of evil and demonism. Every foul, unspeakable corruptible act and thought breeds and is born there deep in its dank, darkness—

An abyss of evil incarnate. It is a real place. If a fiendishly, horrific nightmare could produce a horrifying and inextinguishable nightmare, it would be the functional description of hell.

Jesus was crucified, shed his blood, died on the Cross and went to hell for all people, even those who refuse to acknowledge or follow him. He did it for every nation, every religion, and agnostics, atheists, unbelievers—everyone. He died for the sins of every person in the world then and now to save us from the experience of an unending, eternal nightmare of hell. He loved us so much he took our place there and experienced its every agony. This was necessary for him to complete his mission. Matthew 12:40 testifies,

"For as Jonas was three days and three nights in the whale's belly; so shall the Son of man be three days and three nights in the heart of the earth." However, it did not take Jesus three days just to take the keys of hell and death. He ministered to the Old Testament saints that were there in "Abraham's Bosom." What do you think Jesus ministered to them, salvation perhaps?

> In the Holy Bible, the expression "the Bosom of Abraham" is found only in two verses of St. Luke's Gospel (16:22–23) … in the unseen world of the dead the souls of the righteous occupied an abode or compartment of their own which was distinctly separated by a wall or a chasm from the abode or compartment to which the souls of the wicked were consigned. The latter was a place of torments usually spoken of as Gehenna (cf. Matthew 5:29, 30;18:9; Mark 9:42 sqq. in the Latin Vulgate)—the other, a place of bliss and security known under the names of "Paradise" (cf. Luke 23:43) and "the Bosom of Abraham" (Luke 16:22–23). (Gigot 1907)

He suffered hell for each of us. The Bible does not say what took place there during the three days, but for Jesus to pay the total price for our sin, he had to suffer the accursed physical pain, mental anguish, and the worst agonies of hell. On the cross, Jesus said, "It is finished." He meant that hell as a final destination for our souls was no longer a place we would have to experience. We are victorious in his resurrection because of all he accomplished by his blood sacrifice and death.

The Bible tells the story of his resurrection from hell and his triumph over satan and death. Death is the payment for sin, but we have the esteemed honor and privilege of eternal life with God. Death and hell no longer have any power over us. Thank God for the blood!

Jesus was not resurrected to heaven; he came back to earth first. Our Scripture witness Acts 2:31 testifies, "He seeing this before spake of the resurrection of Christ, that his soul was not left in hell, neither his flesh did see corruption." Even though Jesus had died a horrible death for our sin, horribly beaten and mutilated, his flesh was not corrupted; or decayed and he came back in the flesh with scars in his hands, feet, and side. He demonstrated his victory and used this as evidence to convince his disciples that he was a resurrected body. My surgical scars represent all he accomplished for me by his blood sacrifice and death.

Some have written books as assignments from God about what they witnessed in hell firsthand. Everyone, believer or not, should read Bill Wiese's *23 Minutes in Hell* or Mary K. Baxter's *A Divine Revelation of Hell*. Hopefully, they will scare the hell out of you. We do not have to go there; we can choose.

It saddens me to know that some may be there due to ignorance of the Word and the reality of hell. But if you read this book, you cannot plead ignorance any longer. I am not an authority on the subject, however; only the Bible is .Jesus blood sacrifice was to save us from Hell and an eternity of torment beyond comprehension The grave is a better option than hell. John Piper mentioned in Bill Wiese's book,

> I know of no one who has overstated the terror of Hell ... We are meant to tremble and feel dread. We are meant to recoil from the reality. Not by denying it, but fleeing from it into the arms of Jesus, who died to save us from it. (Wiese 2006)

You can be saved from hell only one way—by receiving Jesus in your heart. Please save yourself from an eternity of hell. Say this prayer.

> Dear Lord Jesus,
>
> I don't want to live eternally in hell. You have made yourself a blood sacrifice for me so I don't have to go there. I confess I am a sinner. I repent and will live the rest of my life in an intimate relationship with you, the Lord of my life and my blood covering. I believe you are the Son of God. Thank you for taking my punishment, dying on the cross for my

sins, then rising up again, triumphing over death and hell. I accept you as my Lord and Savior and trust in your blood sacrifice for my salvation, amen.

If you have said this prayer and believe it in your heart, congratulations! I will look forward to spending an eternity in heaven, not hell, with you. If only one person accepts Jesus as Lord and Savior because of reading this book, it will have served its purpose well. The blood of Jesus indeed has the power to keep us from an eternity in hell.

CHAPTER 8

GOD'S REDEMPTIVE PLAN

Being justified freely by his grace through the redemption
that is in Christ Jesus; Whom God hath set forth to
be a propitiation through faith in his blood.

—Romans 3:24–25

Redemption is "the purchase of God's favor by the death and suffering of Christ; the ransom or deliverance of sinners from the bondage of sin and the penalty of God's violated law by the atonement by Christ's blood" (Webster n.d.). Dake's definition is,

> In short, redemption means that he who is capable of redeeming and taking the place of another or others actually meets the demands of the law and becomes the legal substitute by paying the redemptive price for those who are condemned to death because of breaking the law (sin) In the case of man, satan caused

him to rebel against God and break His law (sin) incurring the death penalty. Man being under the sentence of death could not pay his own death penalty. He also could not live again to enjoy freedom from sin and carryout the eternal purpose for which he was created. To carry out the eternal plan he had to be redeemed and brought back into full reconciliation with God in order to fulfill the holy and righteous demands of the law and holiness of God. God undertook redemption work for man by sending Jesus Christ to die for and resurrect him from the dead so that the original plan could be realized. (Dake 1996)

To begin to understand God's redemptive plan, we must understand the word and concept of redeemed or redemption. Usually to redeem indicates that you have something that belong to you, which is no longer in your possession and you must purchase or buy it back with a sufficient medium of exchange. You may have left a diamond ring at a pawnshop in exchange for money. To get it back, you must pay the money back. Adam was given the earth; God had given him dominion over it. In his fall, he lost it to satan who then became the god of the world. Adam in a sense pawned the earth to satan. Genesis 2:15 reads, "And the LORD God took the man, and put him into the garden of

Eden to dress it and to keep it." God continued with Adam's dominion in Genesis 1:26, 28.

> And God said, Let us make man in our image, after our likeness: and let them have dominion over the fish of the sea, and over the fowl of the air, and over the cattle, and over all the earth, and over every creeping thing that creepeth upon the earth … And God blessed them, and God said unto them, Be fruitful, and multiply, and replenish the earth, and subdue it: and have dominion over the fish of the sea, and over the fowl of the air, and over every living thing that moveth upon the earth.

Dominion is "power to direct, control, use and dispose of at pleasure; right of possession … sovereign or supreme authority; the power of governing and controlling" (Webster n.d.). Adam exchanged his dominion for the knowledge of good and evil. Satan said in Genesis 3:5, "For God doth know that in the day ye eat thereof, then your eyes shall be opened, and ye shall be as gods, knowing good and evil." Due to this "medium of exchange", three things happened:

1. God declares in Genesis 3:22 that Adam has to leave everything—his home and all of the things that God had provided for him;

2. The devil, or satan become the god of this world; and

3. The high price of this exchange included interest—sin, as this was how, when, and where sin entered into the earth.

Romans 5:12, testifies "Wherefore, as by one man sin entered into the world, and death by sin; and so death passed upon all men, for that all have sinned."

Genesis 3:15 is the beginning of the redemptive process. Humanity died spiritually immediately in the exchange, but God set in motion his plan to redeem humanity. In a sense, Adam was given a pawn ticket but would never be able (afford) to redeem it because of the interest—sin and death. God had a plan to redeem all that was lost by Adam to satan, including eternal life (Genesis 2:16–17), the earth as it originally was (Genesis 3:8), the presence of God (Genesis 3:8), freedom from the curse (Genesis 3:17), and dominion over earth (Genesis 1:26). Sin was the interest/penalty that only a sinless man could pay. The redemption had to be by blood because life is in the blood. As we continue to review the redemptive plan of God, it is important that we include the topics of atonement, election, predestination, and Jesus Christ, the Passover Lamb.

Atonement

Atonement express a quality of redemption; according to Vine, Unger, and White, it is "translated from the Greek word Katallage" (1985). Atonement has several definitions. Webster's defines it as "satisfaction given for wrong doing [sin], etc., expiation; theologically, the reconciliation to God by man by means of Jesus sufferings and death" (Guralnik 1982). To have a thorough understanding of this definition, I will define *expiate* as follows: "to appease; make amends for; (wrong doing, guilt [sin]; to suffer for," "Expiation" 1984).

No matter where we go with this topic, it all comes back to the blood sacrifice of Jesus. As we try to wrap our heads around the concept of God's redemptive plan, we must understand the meaning of the words often used interchangeably to explain the process: *salvation*, *atonement*, *expiation*, and *reconciliation*. Redemption is God's plan to return us to our former position or place with him as it was before Adam's fall. However, redemption cannot be expressed all encompassing with mere words; it involves the unconditional love God has for us individually.

Election and Predestination

The doctrines of election and predestination were essential to God's redemptive plan. This discussion will only be in the context of God's omniscience power. It is not intended to be a theocratic or theological thesis on the topic of election and predestination because than can lead to too much debate and distraction from this book topic. The Bible includes many accounts of people God used to carry out the plan in addition to Jesus. It was predestined by God who these people would be, as well as how they would play their roles. God controlled and timed everything. Hebrews 4:12 tells us,

> For the word of God is quick, and powerful, and sharper than any two-edged sword, piercing even to the dividing asunder of soul and spirit, and of the joints and marrow, and is a discerner of the thoughts and intents of the heart.

Every incident, place, and person involved is not by chance but by the election and predestination of the sovereign and divine will of God. It was his perfect plan without any surprises, mistakes, or alterations even every drop of Jesus' blood was anticipated and counted by God.

The plan was incapable of being thwarted, stopped or canceled, even Jesus, a second person of the Godhead with the power of the same, could not prevent it from coming to pass. Jesus declared, "Not my will but thine be done" (Luke 22:42). God's foreordained plan was accomplished by Jesus' blood..

Our Scripture witnesses 1 Peter 1:2, 2 Timothy 1:9–10, Titus 1:2, and Revelation 13:8b relate to the foreknowledge of God before the beginning of time; the plan of salvation was foreordained before the world was created. Satan was a fool to think he was in charge. It was not his victory by any means; it was his death sentence. That may be why there is no indication in the Bible as to where he was specifically at the time of Jesus' crucifixion.

To comprehend this, we must understand the sovereign choice of God in election and predestination, which originate in the divine decision based on God's eternal omniscience of all possible plans of actions. The order logically, not chronologically, is an omniscience-derived decision (election and predestination) and foreknowledge. Election and predestination will be explained further as we in our finite minds attempt to understand God's omniscience.

> Election is summarized this way. In both testaments the Hebrew and Greek words are rendered "elect" "election" "choose" and "chosen." In all cases they mean simply chosen or to choose and are used both in human and divine choices. (1) The latter use election is (a) corporate as of the nation of Israel or of the church (Isaiah 45:4); Ephesians 1:4 and (b) individual as in 1 Peter 1:2; (2) election is according to the foreknowledge of God and wholly by grace, apart from human merit; 1 Corinthians 1:27–28. (Scofield 1996)

Predestination means to mark out or determine beforehand. In scripture this idea is more inclusive than election (chose). The latter is always limited to those specially chosen of God. To say that God predestined the evil acts of men does not mean that he caused these acts or this would make God the author of evil. Rather it means that God foreknowing how men will act under various circumstances determined beforehand to permit them as to act; thus making the acts certain to come to pass, as parts of his total plan, yet leaving all men fully responsible for what they do. (Scofield 1996)

All who acted in concert to kill Jesus were either elected or predestined by the sovereign will of God; it came to pass as part of God's plan. Luke 18:31 testifies, "All things that are written by the prophets concerning the Son of man shall be accomplished." This will lead into our discussion on prophecies. Vine, Unger, and White state,

Prophecies signify the speaking forth of the mind and council of God. It is a declaration, which cannot be known by natural means. The forth-telling of the will of God may make reference to the past, the present or the future. The message of the prophet was a direct revelation of the mind of God for an occasion or situation. The message of the teacher is gathered from the completed revelation contained in the scriptures. (1985)

Dake characterizes a prophet

primarily as a preacher of righteousness, indicating this is the key to the interpretation of many prophecies. He is not only foretelling but forth-telling a speaker for God to rebuke, instruct, watch over, and correct.

Speaking, to man unto edification, exhortation and comfort even when there is no predictive element involved. Moses was a prophet for the Israelite, a spokesman from God, to announce the coming of the messiah which led to Messianic Prophecies and the prophetic office. The prophetic office was established by God and indoctrinated into law for the Jewish people to have a person who was in direct communication with God, until the Messiah comes. (Dake 1996)

Deuteronomy 18:15 reads, "The LORD thy God will raise up unto thee a Prophet from the midst of thee, of thy brethren, like unto me; unto him ye shall hearken," which is also a prophecy of Christ's coming. Acts 7:37 testifies, "A prophet shall the Lord your God raise up unto you of your brethren, like unto me; him shall ye hear."

The roles of a prophet and a priest were different; a priest approaches God on behalf of men by means of sacrifices, while a prophet comes to people as an ambassador from God beseeching them to turn from their evil ways.

> In the case of the Old Testament prophecies, their messages were very largely the proclamation of the divine purposes of salvation and glory to be accomplished in the future. The prophesying of the New Testament prophets were both a preaching of the divine counsel of grace already accomplished and the foretelling of the purposes of God in the future. (Vine, Unger, and White 1985)

Our Scripture witness Hebrews 1:1–2 testifies,

> God, who at sundry times and in divers manners spake in time past unto the fathers by the prophets, Hath in these last days spoken unto us by his Son, whom he hath appointed heir of all things, by whom also he made the worlds.

According to 1 Peter 2:21, "For the prophecy came not in old time by the will of man: but holy men of God spake as they were moved by the Holy Ghost." No prophecy was ever made by an act of human will but by men moved by the Holy Spirit.

> Dr. Hugh Ross, world-renowned astrophysicist, says that approximately 2000 of 2500 prophecies which appear in the Bible have been fulfilled to the letter with no errors (the remaining 500 concern events which have not yet occurred).

> According to Dr. Ross, the probability of any one of the prophecies coming true is less than one in ten. The chances of all 2000 prophecies could have been without error is less than one in 10 to the 2000th power. Since any probability greater than 10 to the 50th power is considered impossible, there is only one reasonable explanation for the complete accuracy of the Bible prophecies: God made them. And God fulfilled them. (Bickle and Jantz 1999)

Jesus Christ, the Passover Lamb of God

The most significant thing about the blood sacrifice of Jesus as the Lamb of God, the fact that it was God's will, is overshadowed by the event itself.

The historical background of 1,500 years and account of the Lord's Passover can be found in Exodus 12:1-29. I will summarize the events here. The Lord spoke to Moses giving in very specific and detailed instructions. Moses as the prophet for the Israelite people was to carry these instructions back to them, to all the congregations of Israel.

He told them that on the 10th day of the month of Nisan every man should take a lamb for his house or family. This lamb was to be observed for five days to ensure that it without any spot or blemish; it was to be male of the first year. They were to keep this lamb for fourteen days and the whole congregation of Israel was to kill their lamb in the evening of the fourteenth day.

The Bible continues, when the lamb is killed that they should take its blood, caught in a container and use hyssop to cover the two-side post and upper doorpost of their houses. They were instructed to cover the entire entrance of the house with the blood of the lamb. The Hebrew day has been determined to begin in the evening at approximately six o' clock. They had to kill their lambs at about three o'clock to have the meal ready before six o' clock.

Following the explicit direction given by the Lord, Moses told the people to stay inside their houses; none were to go out the door until morning. The Lord explains that the Lord will pass through to kill the Egyptians; however when he sees the blood on your doors as he instructed, the Lord will pass over the door, and will not allow the destroyer to come in your house and kill you (Exodus 12:23).

According to the Lord's instruction regarding preparation and cooking the lamb, the Bible says that the entire lamb was to be roasted and eaten. Nothing should be left over for the next day. Also, with the preparation, roasting and eating of the lamb they were instructed not to break any of its bones. "To roast a lamb according to these instructions required that the lamb be placed on a spit shaped like a crossbar so that the body could be spread out." (Booker 2009) Usually, a spit was placed through the head to the tail end and thru the front legs, giving the lamb the shape resembling the cross.

The Passover became a memorial to mark the Hebrew deliverance from Egypt. According to the word of the Lord, as it is the sacrifice of the of the Lord's Passover that protected the people of Israel and it will be an ordinance for them forever. Just as for us today the blood of the lamb saved the people of Israel, the blood of Jesus saves us; as he is our Passover lamb. (Exodus 12:1-23)

> Booker provides the following information about how the Jesus fulfilled his place as the Lamb of God. As the time approached for Jesus to die, He deliberately arranged His literary and personal activities around the events associated with the selection, testing, and death of the Passover Lamb. Jesus was set aside to be sacrificed, examined and crucified on the exact month, day, and hour that the Jews had been handling the lambs

for 1,500 years in keeping with the Feast of the Passover. Josephus, a first century Jewish historian, reported that there were about 256,500 lambs killed in Jerusalem the year Jesus was crucified. At the exact hour when the Jews were preparing their lambs for sacrifice, Jesus was nailed to the cross. (2009)

Our scripture witness Mark 15:25 testifies, and it was the third hour (nine o' clock in the morning Jewish time) and they crucified him.

Thank God for the blood sacrifice of Jesus Christ, our Passover Lamb!

CHAPTER 9

CRUCIFIXION BEFORE THE CROSS, PART I

*Behold, we go up to Jerusalem; and the Son of man shall
be betrayed unto the chief priests and unto the scribes,
and they shall condemn him to death, And shall deliver
him to the Gentiles to mock, and to scourge, and to
crucify him: and the third day he shall rise again.*
—Matthew 20:18–19

In the above passage, Jesus spoke to his disciples about the humiliation and the death he would suffer. He knew what was going to happen to him. The act of the blood sacrifice was God's saving grace for man. The scourging and crucifixion of Jesus were the most supreme sacrifices of all time. Our hearts should be shrines to the act of his giving his life for us; each drop of blood, each wrenching pain, and each torn piece of his flesh was for us all. His blood was given for us wholly, separately, and individually. Relive if you can his death and crucifixion in your mind and spirit. Realize that the blood of Jesus representing his death is a gift to us.

Even though his divinity did not leave him, he did not rely on it to save him. He was as much still God as he was man. However, only his human nature was consumed by his extremely, torturous death. On the cross and in the midst of the slaughter, Jesus could have called on legions of angels to do battle. Matthew 26:53 testifies, "Thinkest thou that I cannot now pray to my Father, and he shall presently give me more than twelve legions of angels?" He could have commanded the angels to destroy the world and every living thing that came against him.

Before the world was created, Jesus knew he would be nailed to a cross, but he also knew he would be a willing Lamb of God to take away sin, including those committed by the people actively involved in his death. His death sentence was because divine law declared repeatedly in the Bible, "the wages of sin is death." We are bought with a price, the blood of Jesus. We are indebted to God; we owe him at the very least our reasonable service of honoring, respecting, and esteeming his sacrifice. There is no remission of sin without blood. God's ordained law and divine plan required it.

Dear Father,

Thank you for the blood sacrifice of Jesus. I will always honor and esteem this redemptive act of the Trinitarian Godhead. I will burn the

> memory of what it represents into my heart
> and spirit. I will live my life giving glory,
> praise, and worship to a God who is alive and
> who has kept me from an eternity in hell. All
> things that represent prosperity in my life—
> healing, protection, emotional wholeness,
> and financial stability—are direct results of
> the precious blood sacrifice of Jesus, amen.

I have read books about how people experienced heaven and hell. By my spirit, I wanted to experience being at the scene of Jesus' scourging and crucifixion. I could then allow you to experience this journey to get a vision of what it was really like to be there. Try to see it through my eyes as I have written it here, by your spirit.

Luke 18:31 testifies, "Then he took unto him the twelve, and said unto them, Behold, we go up to Jerusalem, and all things that are written by the prophets concerning the Son of man shall be accomplished."

Jesus made many journeys on earth as the Word made flesh. The most significant one was Capernaum to Jerusalem. Keller stated that it could be traced without difficulty to the saving grace of mankind—his last journey through Palestine. The trip from Capernaum to Jerusalem was a journey to pay the wages of sin. It is estimated it took three days to make this journey on foot from Galilee to Jerusalem. Jesus went by the borders of Judea and beyond Jordan (Mark 10:31), crossed the Jordan, and arrived in Jericho (Luke

19:1). From Jericho to Jerusalem is twenty-three miles of old, dusty, dry road weaving around and between elevated cliffs reaching heights of 4,000 feet, nearing the Mount of Olives. He may have spent the night in Jericho at the house of the Jewish tax collector Zacchaeus according to Luke 19:2 (Keller 1956).

Luke 19:41 testifies, "And when he was come near, he beheld the city, and wept over it." Jesus by his divine Spirit had some inclination or insight of what was going to happen there. Halley pointed out that the journey from Jerusalem to Gethsemane was about a mile. He reached Coenaculum, the name of the traditional place of the upper room, the scene of the Last Supper. Some historians thought that this was possibly the home of Mary, the mother of Mark. From there, about 8 p.m. or 9 p.m. in the evening, he traveled to Gethsemane. It is at this point in his journey that he experienced the beginning agony of his passion (Halley 1962).

In the garden of Gethsemane, he was in agony for two to four hours. Our Scripture witness Luke 22:44 testifies, "And being in an agony he prayed more earnestly: and his sweat was as it were great drops of blood falling down to the ground." Mark 14:34 testifies, "And saith unto them, My soul is exceeding sorrowful unto death: tarry ye here, and watch." We can hear him, if we listen by our spirit to the desperation and hopelessness of his situation. Jesus prayed to his Father as his humanity cried out in anguish. In agony, he prayed more earnestly, and his sweat was like great drops of blood falling to the ground. Luke 22:43 testifies, "And there appeared an angel unto him from heaven, to strengthen him."

I am reminded of Hebrews 12:4: "Ye have not yet resisted unto blood, striving against sin." Jesus understood the reason he was suffering and would die was to save us from our sins. Jesus experienced hematidorsis; Tabor explained that means the excretion of blood or blood pigment in the sweat caused by extreme stress (2013).

As his intense suffering began, satan came on the scene in the heart of Judas. The stage was set for God's plan for eternal life. Luke 22:3 testifies, "Then entered satan into Judas." Judas betrays Jesus. For Jesus the incomparable tragedy begins. Matthew 26:56 testifies that right after Jesus was arrested, "all the disciples forsook him, and fled." The very people who were seemly, so dedicated to his cause, the same group who "took up his cross to follow him," his people, those he loved and trusted deserted him! These are they who had just a few hours before swore allegiance to him. Wasn't it Peter who had just said at the Last Supper, "I will lay down my life for you? Can you imagine Jesus' intense feeling of betrayal?

This turn of events must have devastated Jesus. He must have been heartbroken. This may be why he tells us, "I will never leave you or forsake you." He even assures us he will heal the brokenhearted. He experienced being brokenhearted firsthand. He knows how badly it hurts. Heartbreak causes physical pain. We must remember in our times of excruciating heartache that he took the pain of heartbreak and sorrows to the cross with him. We need to accept his blood sacrifice as healing for our broken hearts.

At times in our lives, husbands, wives, friends, children, or loved ones will leave us or turn on us, but we can be comforted by the fact that Jesus took on that emotional pain for us so we do not have to bear it alone; it is covered by his blood. All we need to do is develop an intimate relationship with him. He will step up to the plate in every situation. He promised us he would not leave us comfortless. The Holy Spirit is our comforter, a gift to our souls—mind, will, and emotions.

After Jesus arrest, he was brought before the High Council the Sanhedrin, the highest Jewish authority and the highest judicial court of the Jews. It is also interesting to note that the high priest of the council lived near where Jesus had eaten the Last Supper.

Jesus was mocked as he was shuttled back and forth from Pilate to Herod. His first trial included being mocked by the Jews (Luke 22:63–65). He was then sent to Herod and his crowd (Luke 23:11). Then he was taken to Pilates' soldiers. Finally, the chief priest, elders, scribes, and anyone else in the crowd of onlookers got their turn at this madness. Matthew 27:39–56 demonstrated the unspeakable evilness of men. Mocking was as cruel a mental torture as scourging was a physical torture. Think of Jesus having done only good works, never having sinned. Jesus was blatantly disrespected as he lay down his life for mankind. Jesus was kept from midnight to daylight. He was humiliated, mocked, and denied by Peter, and at daylight, he was sentenced by the Jews and sent to Pilate.

The Roman soldiers playing one of their favorite gambling games, "King," joined in to enjoyed humiliating and mocking Jesus, who became the game of the day.

> It was played with sheep's knuckles as dice and they would roll those dice on a playing board. The soldiers would pick one of their own and make him the "king." They would give him robe, a crown, a scepter, and they would pay homage to him. During the course of the day the soldiers would gamble for all of his possessions—clothes, wife, home back in Rome, etc., culminating in gambling for who got to kill him. These Roman soldiers would pick some poor hapless new recruit and they'd make a game out of killing him ... Now enter the condemned prisoner, the rabbi Jesus. He was made to look like a king by being given a robe, a crown, and a scepter. He was then mocked, beaten, spit upon, while they pretended to pay homage to him. Eventually all of his belongings were gambled on as they "cast lots" which was done with sheep's knuckle dice and they killed him. (Prather 2009, June 18)

Isaiah 50:6 testifies, "I gave my back to the smiters, and my cheeks to them that plucked off the hair: I hid not my face from shame and spitting." "The Hebrew word for *pluck* in verse 6 is *maw-rat,* which in this verse means to make bald" (Cocherell February 10, 2008). The *Jewish Encyclopedia* states, "To mutilate another by cutting or shaving is, consequently, considered a great disgrace" ("Beard" 2008). Any insult to a beard was the last outrage an enemy could inflict (2 Samuel 10:4–5; Isaiah 50:6). One of the greatest humiliations performed by a conqueror was to shave or pluck the beards of their captives. It was a demonstration of disrespect and defacement (Cocherell February 10, 2008). The Romans were aware of the fact that wearing a beard was no insignificant matter for an Israelite man. Cocherell stated,

> The beard was to be a constant reminder of his status as a citizen of the Creator God's holy nation. Every pious Israelite man also believed that his beard represented his obedience to God command, and that to voluntarily deface it was a form of rebellion against God and his law. (February 10, 2008)

The Bible teaches that both respect and disrespect can be shown by treatment of a man's beard. Cocherell continued,

> Wearing of full beard was a sign of masculinity, physical maturity, honor and dignity. To have the beard forcibly removed, ripped off or defaced could be considered symbolic of judgment, punishment, disgrace and humiliation, all of which Jesus suffered for us. (Cocherell February 10, 2008)

To humiliate Jesus further, he was spat upon with venomously regurgitated spit.

> To spit and spittle were considered a source of legal defilement, to spit in one's face was regarded as the grossest insult. It was barbarically, disgustingly grotesque. (Numbers 12–14; Deuteronomy 25:9; Isaiah 50:6; Matthew 26:67 and 27:30). (Unger and Harrison 1998)

Indeed, it was a great indignity to spit toward anyone and is still considered so today.

I imagine Jesus, the spotless Lamb, in a state of shock, being subjected to the vilest forms of degradation. Jesus may have suffered hypovolemic shock from blood and fluid loss, traumatic shock caused by injuries, and cardiogenic shock, which occurs when the heart fails to pump blood. However, Jesus never lost his sensibilities (*How He Died* 2006). Before he gave up the ghost, he was alert and coherent enough to make clear and astounding statements.

Jesus had been just two days before anointed (the third time) with oil from the alabaster box. I understand the connection; Jesus talked about it in our Scripture witnesses Matthew 26:7, 10, and 12–13.

> There came unto him a woman having an alabaster box of very precious ointment, and poured it on his head, as he sat at meat.

> When Jesus understood it, he said unto them, "Why trouble ye the woman? for she hath wrought a good work upon me. she did it for my burial."

> For in that she hath poured this ointment on my body, she did it for my burial. Verily I say unto you, Wheresoever this gospel shall be preached in the whole world, there shall also this, that this woman hath done, be told for a memorial of her.

This was the only anointing for his burial Jesus recognized though he had been anointed with oil on two other occasions (Luke 7:38; John 12:3). This is significant; when the women came to the tomb to complete the task of anointing Jesus, as was the custom for Jewish burials they found the tomb empty. There was a divine purpose for the woman and her

Rita Y. Jarrett

alabaster box of ointment to anoint him for his burial as well as for the humiliation, degradation, and shame he would suffer. God will always provide "a ram in a bush."

During his trail, Jesus claimed to be (who he is) the Messiah; the Jews regarded that as a claim he was a king, the Son of God, and because of this statement the Sanhedrin, a Jewish judicial body, claimed it to be sufficient ground for condemning him to death, (the wages of sin), on the trumped-up charge of blasphemy.

According to existing law, the sentence had to be confirmed by the Roman procurator. Only he could authorize the death penalty, (for the wages of sin). The procurator of Judea at that time was Pontius Pilate. He was a despicable, loathsome, corrupted character; he was considered cruel and hardhearted and hated the Jews, which they well knew. The scourging or beating of Jesus took place at the pavement in Pilate's court.

After this, Jesus would be was seized by Roman soldiers to complete the sentence of crucifixion. However, while still inside the court buildings, the Roman soldiers began the shameful humiliation of Jesus. They vented their hatred and disdain on Jesus and "clothed him with purple robe and platted a crown of thorns forcing it unto his head causing blood gushing and a tortured look on His face" (Mark 15:17).

The crown of thorns' spiritual purpose was to take on ever-psychological illness or disorder. When the crown was forced on his head, the spikes irritated or penetrated the trigeminal lobes in the front of the head as well as the greater occipital lobes in the back of the head [for my sins]. Jesus suffered an inordinate, immense amount of pain starting from the head and spreading throughout the whole body [for my sins]. (*How He Died* 2006)

This source also shares that he was beaten on the head with reeds to further crush and split open the skin, exposing his skull. Because of the numerous blood vessels about the head and face there must have been a profuse amount of bleeding from these wounds (*How He Died* 2006).

Jesus was possibly flogged once by the Jews and then scourged by the Romans. These were two extremely different types of beatings (Matthew 26:65; John 19:1).

Talmudic law not only made detailed provision for the manner in which floggings were to be carried out, but also altered the concept of the biblical punishment; the maximum of 40 lashes was reduced to 39 (Mak. 22a), so as to avoid the danger of exceeding 40 even by mistake; and the offenses which carried the punishment of flogging were exactly defined, depriving it of its character as a residuary and omnibus punishment. The number of 39 lashes became the standard rather than the maximum number; but in order to prevent death by flogging—which would amount to a violation of the biblical injunction of "not more" than flogging—the person to be flogged was first physically examined in order to determine the number of lashes that could safely be administered to him (Mak. 3:11). ("Flogging," 2008)

Lambrianides points out that "according to Jewish custom, a prisoner was flogged 39 times (40 minus 1 was a sign of Jewish mercy)" (n.d.). However, due to their blatant disrespect for Jesus' true identity and their desire to see him dead, the Jews may have disregarded this law as well.

"Floggings were administered with a whip made of calfskin on the bare upper body of the offender —one third of the lashes being given on the breast and the other two thirds on the back" ("Flogging" 2008). This was the Jewish rule. However, Jesus was sentenced under Roman law, and that law had no limit (*How He Died* 2006). There could have been as many as a hundred lashes or more. The Roman used lictors to perform the scourgings. They would usually use two lictors but sometimes as many as four to six. Typically, the Romans would strip the prisoner and bind him to a low pillar or the prisoner would be bent over it or chained to an upright pillar so as to be stretched out.

Scourging was done with whip called a flagrum and consisted of a handle with two or three short thongs attached, usually of leather. Knotted at intervals along the thongs and at the ends were small pieces of metal, glass, bone, or other hard object. The flagrum was primarily designed to cause bruising. The punishment was administered by Roman soldiers known as lictors. A lictor received special training for this duty and knew how to wield the flagrum so as to open existing bruises and cause the blood to flow freely. More than one lictor was used to scourge each prisoner. They were trained so they could inflict blows simultaneously upon the shoulders, back, buttocks and legs. Under Roman law there was no limit to the number of lashes. The only limitation was when the centurion in charge determined that further punishment would result in death. There were occasions, even when the victim fainted, if the lictor could feel his pulse and determine he was breathing the beating would continue. Because scourging was normally preparatory to crucifixion its object was to weaken the prisoner to the point of collapse and to bring him as near death as possible. Extensive blood loss was most likely intended to shorten the victim's time on the cross.

The lictors, taking great pleasure in seeing the rupture of bruises as the flagrums tore them open and blood oozed, spurted and then flowed down Jesus' body and legs to form an every expanding crimson pool about his feet. His entire backside quickly became a bloody mass of ripped and torn flesh. The metal and bone particles cut deeper and deeper into the muscle [down to the bone] until strips of flesh tore loose. (Bennett 2011)

So violent was the beating that a mist of blood formed in the air, and even as the mist of Jesus blood fell, it became a blood covering for our sins.

As I imagine each piece of his flesh being gouged out, each jagged gash bringing more of a mist, I am reminded of the mist that arose in the beginning. Genesis 2:6 testifies, "But there went up a mist from the earth, and watered the whole face of the ground." Our Lord Jesus was beaten so brutally and sadistically that his blood too covered the face of the ground. It was the punishment that fit the crime of our sins and the sins of the world. We can see a connection that runs through the Bible about God's plan in the beginning to affect his plan in the end. Genesis 2:7 continues on the same thing: "And the Lord God formed man of the dust of the ground, and breathed into his nostrils the breath of life; and man became a living soul."

Isaiah 52:14 testifies, "As many were astonished at thee; his visage was so marred more than any man, and his form more than the sons of men." Jesus was unrecognizable as a man; he had been beaten into pieces, crumbled because of our sin. The pain Jesus suffered was for our sins. The blood he lost was for our healing . I imagine him being bruised for our iniquities; the chastisement of my peace is upon him and with his stripes I am healed (Isaiah 53:4–5). This Scripture speaks of his bruising. The Hebrew word *daka* means "to crumble; transitively, to bruise (literally or figuratively) ... beat to pieces, break (in pieces), bruise, contrite, crush, destroy, humble, oppress, smite" (*Strong's Concordance* n.d.). I believe that smitten refers to stripes by scourging. This proves that this was part of the work of atonement for which his blood was shed. It was by this particular phase of punishment that our bodily healing was provided.

After this scourging, a brutal, barbaric beating, Jesus began the trip to Golgotha.

> The Via Dolorosa, literally "sorrowful way," is the traditional route of Jerusalem, which our Lord traveled on the day of His crucifixion from the judgment seat of Pilate, also called the Praetorium (Matthew 27:2–26) to the place of his crucifixion on Mount Calvary. (Houdmann 2008)

It is still the way Franciscans guide pilgrimages that follow Jesus' final journey.

Jesus Christ endured an hour-long walk of perhaps up to two miles while carrying weight of the horizontal part of the cross on his shoulders that pressed into his open wounds. He did it for us.

This part of the cross,

> the patibulum, was usually unfinished timber wood, very rough, weighting between 70–120 pounds and was meant be used over and over again. Normally victims carried the patibulum naked for the hour's walk. (*How He Died* 2006)

The cross Jesus carried was like the sin he carried. It once belonged to someone else. It was not unusual for the Romans to use the cross over and over again for different victims.

> The Romans when there were multiple victims, would tie their ankles together to decrease the chances of them trying to run away. When one fell they all would fall Jesus … was clothed in a garment during this time he would be stripped again when he arrived at Golgotha. (*How He Died* 2006)

They arrived at Golgotha, "the place of the skull," at the third hour, perhaps 9 a.m. (*How He Died* 2006). As Jesus climbed Golgotha, he was probably met with a tremendous odor and a chilling site.

> Golgotha was a place outside the city where it was not unusual for the citizen to bring the criminals and orphans who died to be eaten by the rats and birds of prey ... the ground would have been muddy from the dirt and blood of other victims and the place was probably littered with rotting corpses, rats, maggots, flies and flesh eating birds. (*How He Died* 2006)

The flesh-eating birds would have been gouging at the open, bleeding flesh of Jesus as he hung on the cross. This was a sewer of mutilated, decaying bodies. This visual was an intentional and significant part of the ghastly horror and gruesomeness of the crucifixion. It has been recorded that "when archaeologist excavated such places in 1890, the stench was so great that they had to take 15 minutes shifts in order not to pass out" (*How He Died* 2006).

CHAPTER 10

CRUCIFIXION ON THE CROSS. THE FINAL ACT, PART II

And they crucified him, and parted his garments,
casting lots: that it might be fulfilled which was spoken
by the prophet, They parted my garments among
them, and upon my vesture did they cast lots.

—Matthew 27:35

Jesus was dropped at the foot of the cross, was stripped again, and laid down on the patibulum. The nails, which were "made of heavy iron material, probably square, and 7–9 inches long" (*Jesus Nails* 2002), were driven through his wrists. Though there has always been debate over the weight, size, and number of nails used, the fact remains that Jesus was nailed to the cross, and this excruciating process caused more blood loss. According to Lambrianides, crucifixion was one of the most painful, cruel, and most humiliating forms of punishment ever devised by man. The Jewish historian Josephus describes it "the most wretched of deaths," and Seneca argues that suicide is preferable to the cruel fate of being put on the cross. Roman citizens were exempt from crucifixion except in cases of treason. Cicero called it "crudelissimum taeterrimumque supplicium"—a most cruel and disgusting punishment and he further suggested that the very word, cross, should be far removed not only from the person of a Roman citizen, but also from his thoughts, his eyes and ears, and used only in slaves, "Extremum summumque supplicium"—extreme and ultimate punishment of slaves. If the Romans regarded crucifixion with horror so did the Jews. They made no distinction between tree and cross. "Anyone who is hung on a tree is under God's curse." Deut. 21–23, They could not bring themselves to believe that the Messiah would die under a curse. (Lambrianides n.d.)

The method the Romans had perfected ensured that crucifixion victims would hang painfully until their diaphragm went into

> spasm and they literally suffocated to death. (*All About Jesus Christ* 2008)

> He was placed on His back with His arms outstretched. The nails were first driven through small wooden disks to eliminate any chance of the heads pulling through the flesh. The site of the incision in the arm was critical; the Romans had perfected the procedure, a very specific procedure. The legionnaire who had been given the task felt for a specific spot, the nail had to be driven in between the bones of the forearm up close to the wrist while not severing any major arteries or veins. There is a space between eight small bones which is structurally suitable to permit a full body weight to be supported for a time. If the nails had been driven into the palms of the hands, under the extreme weight, they would have ripped out between the fingers. (*All About Jesus Christ* 2008)

They were also able to drive the nails without breaking any bones. It is safe to believe there were nails and this is of no real consequence because had Jesus been glued to the cross the outcome that God planned would have still been the same.

It is depicted that the pain Jesus experienced is unfathomable. The nails tore through muscle and skin causing irritation and rupturing the median nerve, causing causalga, lighting-sharp pain, a sensation spreading throughout the entire body (2006). These same types of seven-inch nails were driven through the feet that some writers say were crossed over each other so one nail would penetrate the nerves of both feet. "The nails placed in the feet were usually placed between the metatarsal bones damaging the digital nerves" (*How He Died* 2006). This would also cause the same type of pain as penetrating the median nerves in the wrist.

> Crucifixion is slow process of, among other things, suffocation (more properly, asphyxiation—the choking on your breath). In order to inhale the victim had to hang by the nails in their wrists. However, to exhale, the victim had to transfer their weight from their wrists to their feet pushing on the nail in their feet in order to lift themselves up. This constant up and own motion would have caused excruciating pain from the nails, as well as the back rubbing up and down the stipes. The caps of thorns (providing Jesus was still wearing it on the cross, most likely He was since that would add more pain and shame to the Crucifixion) would have been constantly moving on His head by hitting the

stipes. There was no comfort on the cross.
The unnatural position of the body made every
movement painful and greatly interfered with
breathing, especially inhaling, taking a breath
was excruciating, for an attempt at adequate
breathing, it required lifting the body up by
pushing up on the feet and flexing the elbows.
(*How He Died* 2006)

This put all the weight of Jesus' body on the nails in his
feet; the pain had to go beyond the maximum any human
could bear. After the nails were driven through his wrists
and feet, he was hoisted up, and the cross was dropped
crudely into a hole. The pain of the torn flesh and his bruised,
lacerated, naked skin ripped against the rough wood of (our)
cross. This further increased the bleeding and pain.

Even on the Cross, He intercedes asking the Father to
forgive them. The blood cover is now in effect.

The impact of the revelation that comes from this next
action is awesome. The word bow means "to bend the
knee or body or incline the head in reverence, submission,
salutation, recognition, or acknowledgment; to yield and
to submit; to bend or incline the knee, body, or head in
worship, submission, respect, civility, or agreement"
(Webster's New Universal, 1992). Our scripture witness,
John 19:30, testifies "When Jesus therefore had received
the vinegar, he said, It is finished: and HE BOWED HIS
HEAD, and GAVE UP THE GHOST" (Emphasis added).

Our Lord and Savior with his last breathe, He bowed before God, the Father, in reverence with worship and respect to his authority, fully submitted, and in total agreement with his plan to save us from our sin and redeem us back to God.

Jesus did not hang his head in death or shame. He bowed His head in an act of worship and reverence. My God, that is powerful! Jesus gave of himself to the utmost. Who would think that after all He suffered and been through—scourged and crucified on the Cross, that His last effort would be to recognize God in such a demonstration of love and trust. He bowed his head and gave up the ghost. Even after all this, He is still giving. Our scripture witness, John 10:17-18, is fulfilled and testifies, "[17] Therefore doth my Father love me, because I lay down my life, that I might take it again. [18] No man taketh it from me, but I lay it down of myself. I have power to lay it down, and I have power to take it again. This commandment have I received of my Father." He laid down his life and died when He gave up the Ghost.

It is important to remember what was declared in John 19:33–36.

> But when they came to Jesus, and saw that he was dead already, they brake not his legs: But one of the soldiers with a spear pierced his side, and forthwith came there out blood and water. And he that saw it bare record, and his record is true: and he knoweth that he saith true, that ye might believe. For these

things were done, that the scripture should be fulfilled, A bone of him shall not be broken (Exodus 12:46; Numbers 9:12; Psalm 34:20).

This takes me back to one of the pressing questions I had searched for an answer. With Jesus so badly beaten, his body torn and lacerated horribly, what was the concern about his bones being broken? Our scripture witness, Isaiah 52:14, testifies "As many were astonied at thee; his visage was so marred more than any man, and his form more than the sons of men:" Jesus is now unrecognizable as a man. It is paramount to understand that Jesus blood loss must have been hemorrhagic. It is truly amazing that during such mutilating and mangling injuries that not one of His bones is broken as God decreed in John 19:36.

Why was it of such paramount importance that not one of Jesus' bones be broken? Baffling to my finite mind, I asked the Holy Spirit why, and he answered me. As I have said, when Jesus' blood is honored, the Holy Spirit will manifest himself.

As we learned, blood is produced only in bone marrow. How would this affect or impact his bodily resurrection? In order for Jesus to have risen with a fully functional, flesh-and-bone body was, of course, by divine intervention. God knew Jesus would have to have his blood loss replenished just as in any human body. Jesus is still the hypostatic union, even though He has sustained the hemorrhagic blood loss caused by His crucifixion. The bones of his human body held bone marrow, which is where and how blood is restored and replenished in the body. We can recall that Jesus was born a Holy thing in Luke 1:35. His" holy blood" had to be restored from His bone marrow. The bones of the body that God had prepared for Jesus were declared by God to remain intact, and not be broken. Moreover, God could not allow the blood supply of Jesus to be desecrated (Acts 2:27; 13:37).

Scientific evidence has demonstrated that blood can only be replenished in the bone marrow. I reiterate that there is no substitute for blood. Jesus did not have a blood transfusion. Some reader may think this is a preposterous hypothesis. However, when I asked the Holy Spirit, the Spirit of truth, why God had declared that none of Jesus' bones be broken, this is what the Holy Spirit revealed to me. I understand that the answer could be because God just said that no bone in his body would be broken just as God spoke to create everything into existence. Scripture witnesses, including Romans 11:33–34, always supersede scientific evidence. Who can know the mind of God?

Let's review the facts. Jesus gave himself as a blood sacrifice. The Bible tells us that without blood, there is no remission of sin. Jesus died and emptied himself of his blood. He went to hell and was resurrected bodily. Luke 24:34–43 testifies that he was seen and touched. Also, he talked, walked, and ate. Luke 24:39 expressly says that a spirit hath not flesh and bones; Jesus said, "Behold my hands and my feet, that it is I myself: handle me, and see; for a spirit hath not flesh and bones, as ye see me have." Furthermore, Jesus

Rita Y. Jarrett

was seen by 500 witnesses and walked the earth for forty days before he ascended to heaven.

I believe because he did not come back as only a spirit but with a fully functioning body, he needed blood. His bones were not broken because the blood for his body could be reproduced only in his bone marrow. According to the *Encyclopedia of Jewish Medical Ethics*, bone marrow is considered flesh (Steingburg 2003). This may be food for thought. The facts are as follows.

1. The life of the flesh is in the blood (Leviticus 11:17).
2. The Word was made flesh (John 1:14).
3. Jesus body was resurrected not his spirit; his spirit could not die.

Jesus' humiliation continued. He was exposed naked on the cross, not carefully draped as artists portray him. His forced nakedness was another attempt by the executioners to further humiliate ridicule, and shame Jesus. Jewish people were modest in dress and appearance; they kept their bodies covered because they considered the body holy—belonging to God. To be exposed naked in such a way was a shameful humiliation for Jesus.

> *Tz'ni'ut* means modesty, simplicity, a touch of bashfulness, and reserve. But perhaps above these, it signifies privacy. The classical symbol of *tz'ni'ut* is the veil. It bespeaks

privacy, a person apart; Isaiah (3:18) calls it *tif'eret* ("glory"). The principle of *tz'ni'ut* rejects all nudity, not only in public. It is popularly thought to apply primarily to women, but it is a desirable quality in men as well. (Lamm n.d.)

Jesus was aware of and most certainly practiced the *tznuit* principles of modest (Genesis 9:23; 1 Chronicles 19:4–5; 2 Corinthians 5:3; Revelation 16:15).To be openly and fully exposed—naked was considered a disgraceful, desecration of the body. We are temples of the Holy Ghost. The Word also reminds us to be holy, as God is.

Beside enduring pain and blood loss for us, Jesus also endured great humiliation, shame, and heartache. The first Adam was covered with the skin of an animal by God because of sin as indicated in Genesis 3:21: "Unto Adam also and to his wife did the LORD God make coats of skins, and clothed them." The second Adam, Jesus, was uncovered because of sin. Jesus took on the sins of the world to be crucified for our sake. The Word says he became sin for us. The pain and humiliation continued as the punishment to fit the crime, the sins of the world, unfolded.

A sign that read "Jesus of Nazareth, the King of the Jews" was placed above his head in Hebrew, Latin, and Greek.

These were the three prominent languages spoken in Palestine so that all could read it. Hebrew was the national dialect of the Jews; Greek was the universal tongue of the civilized western world; and Latin was the official language of the judicial and executive power of the then ruling empire. Geikie declares that these three languages were a symbol of, "The relationship of the cross to all the nationalities of the world." ("The Crucifixion" n.d.)

Since Jesus died for the sins of the world, I agree. Actually, when Pilate wrote the statement this way, the chief priests were very indignant. John 19–21 testifies, "Then said the chief priest of the Jews to Pilate, Write not, The King of the Jews; but that he said, I am King of the Jews. Pilate answered, "What I have written I have written." "The inscription also included the name of the condemned, his place of residence, and the charge on which he was sentenced to be crucified" ("The Crucifixion" n.d.). Jesus accepted all the mocking, scoffing, and jeering by the high priest, elders, scribes, soldiers, and the great crowd of onlookers cheering for and demanding his death.

Many people would pass in and out of the city and the attention of the crowd would naturally be arrested by the spectacle of the crosses and equally so; they would have been impressed by the Roman *titulus* over the cross of Jesus. His death was a historically despicable spectacle. Jesus suffered intense agony for my sins. Crucifixion was an agonizing spectacle that lasted sometimes up to two days. The persecutors wanted to prolong the spectacle and to delay death in order to extend the torture as long as possible.

His blood flowed without ceasing. His blood was everywhere. His blood was crying out pleading to God for our salvation. It was a blood covered and saturated scene, a hemorrhage of love for us. How can we as Christians not take Jesus' blood sacrifice with more seriousness, study, respect, honor, and esteem? The theme of Jesus' blood runs through the Bible; each passage has blood between the lines.

We must come into a spiritual awareness of its efficacy, divine nature, and power. Get out some of those old blood songs. Get them down in your spirit. Search out the blood Scriptures and imprint them in your mind, heart, and spirit. On every occasion, acknowledge Jesus' blood sacrifice. As you grow and mature in this knowledge, your spiritual life will never be the same.

Blood was not the only essential of the crucifixion; the pain involved cannot be measured or understood. God revealed to us that sin has great pain (Ezekiel 30:15–16.) This is the basis of the pain Jesus knew he would have to endure. He fully understood what he was going to suffer; that was what made him plead and bleed in the garden of Gethsemane. The following discussion of pain is of paramount importance to get a sense of the level of pain Jesus suffered. Pain affects the body as follows according to Potter and Perry.

Nerve receptors on the skin and tissues responds to stimuli resulting from actual or potential tissue damage. The International Association for the Study of Pain (IASP) defined pain as "an unpleasant, subjective sensory and emotional experience associated with actual or potential tissue damage. The pain threshold is reached when a stimulus is intense enough to create a nerve impulse. Superficial or cutaneous pain is pain resulting from stimulation of skin the pain is of short duration and is localized. Pain may be sharp, dull, or unique to organs involved. It produces crushing sensation or a burning sensation. There is also referred and radiating pain. We use pain scales to determine the severity of pain that a person may be experiencing; 0 1 2 3 4 5 6 7 8 9 10 indicating no pain, mild pain, moderate pain severe pain and unbearable pain. Sustained physiological responses to pain could cause serious harm to an individual, and cases of severe traumatic pain could send a person into shock. (Potter and Perry 1993)

Pain anywhere in the body causes distress, and Jesus suffered every type and intensity of pain imaginable. With every sympathetic and parasympathetic symptom, he indeed took our infirmities, our disease, and our pain. It is for this reason Jesus intended us to be free from chronic pain. God created pain receptors in our bodies only as a means to warn us of danger or impending harm. The devil will attempt to pervert this system and have us blame God. We are living beneath our privilege and position in Christ when we fail to acknowledge the fullness of his blood sacrifice. Our Scripture witness Ezekiel 30:15–16 testifies, "I will pour my fury upon **Sin** ... **Sin** shall have great pain." It is interesting that in each verse, *sin* is capitalized. Our Scripture witness Acts 2:24 testifies, "Whom God hath raised up, having loosed the pains of death: because it was not possible that he should be holden of it."

The pain Jesus suffered was as significant as it was excruciating. In the pain he endured, our sickness and disease were destroyed as he became sin for us. Our Scripture witness 1 Peter 2:24 testifies, "Who his own self bare our sins in his own body on the tree, that we, being dead to sins, should live unto righteousness: by whose stripes ye were healed." By his stripes we were healed. The stripes (lashes), affliction or punishment of his flesh, healed the broken and torn places of disease that would attack our bodies. The beating had a divine purpose of producing the pain that represented our healing just as the blood represented our redemption from sin.

The level and degree of the pain was equal to the healing power for every sickness and disease. Healing is in the atonement of Jesus. Leviticus 17:11 testifies, "For the life of the flesh is in the blood: and I have given it to you upon the altar to make an atonement for your souls: for it is the blood that maketh an atonement for the soul." John Lake said, "Sin, sickness and death are the triumvirate of the devil; the triple curse" (*Copeland* 1995). In 1 John 3:8, we read, "For this purpose the Son of God was manifested, that he might destroy the works of the devil" and therefore his triple curse. The excruciating pain and the hemorrhage of blood worked in concert together to forever defeat sin, sickness, and death, and yes, pain!

O' what a mighty God we serve! Yes, the pain was horrific, but so are the sins of the world. The pain Jesus suffered compensated for our sin and for our healing. As cruel as the beating was, God determined it was the only fitting price for divine healing and sin. Divine healing would belong to his children again and forever. Jesus suffered every aspect of pain and to the highest degree a human could suffer pain and still live to die on the cross in order to fulfill every Messianic prophecy.

Imagine the worst and most excruciating pain you have ever experienced. Now multiple that times unbelievable and unbearable you would still not come close to what Jesus suffered for us. Each spasm of pain he suffered was equal to the healing power needed for every sickness and disease. Healing is the atonement.

The wages of sin is death. What Jesus suffered for me will never be determined in this world. He stayed on the cross until he took on himself all sin. I like to think he endured the cross until he finally got to my sins. Thank you, Jesus!

Jesus hung in utter humiliation, shame, and pain for me. He suffered indescribable torture not giving up until he got to me. With every breath, Jesus held out just for me. It was the utmost personal and individualized sacrifice he made for each one of us. He did this unconditionally, whether we acknowledge him or not whether we serve him or not. It was absolutely unconditionally.

Think about it, what drops of his blood did he shed expressly for you? What agony did he endure just for you? It was not finished until it was finished for all of us, including the unborn. He stayed on the cross even while hearing the taunts of the chief priest, scribes, and elders who dared him to come down from the cross. Matthew 27:42 testifies, "He saved others; himself he cannot save. If he be the King of Israel, let him now come down from the cross, and we will believe him." It was not until every last one of us was redeemed that he gave up the ghost. Jesus died for each one of us an individual death. For each person he suffered individual pain and bleeding His love for each person is unconditional and perfect.

Whose sins do you believe he stayed on the cross for until the end? We know he could have given up the ghost any time; maybe he stayed that last five minutes to have your sin put on him. Can you picture Jesus on the cross for you? Can you understand his supreme sacrifice for all of us? Jesus came to destroy the works of the evil one as 1 John

3:8 testifies: "He that committeth sin is of the devil; for the devil sinneth from the beginning. For this purpose the Son of God was manifested, that he might destroy the works of the devil."

He performed the most personal and unselfish act of all for you and me. You must make this personal! It is the most personal, and unselfish act of all creation. Jesus died a billion multiplied deaths so the world would be saved from hell, pain, sickness, sorrow—all the fruit of our sin.

There was darkness from noon until 3:00 p.m. In Jesus' final three hours, he began the final stage of expiation for human sin. What Jesus suffered in the last dreadful hours, we can never know in this world. He stayed on the cross until he got to everyone's sin. I don't know where in the line of all the people my sins stood, but Thank God he stayed in his suffering and waited for me; how long was he in agony for you? You must understand the implications of what I am writing. Jesus did it all for you as though you were the only person in the world. Meditate deeply on this; make it real in the sense that you are able to know you know. Jesus had you, your healing, your life, and the desires of your heart in mind. Jesus loves you!

At the ninth hour, 3:00 in the afternoon, the tragedy for the wages of sin, death, came to an end.

CHAPTER 11

WE ARE COVERED BY THE BLOOD OF JESUS

And they overcame him by the blood of the
Lamb. And the words of their testimony.

—Revelation 12:11

God is love. His heart blood is Jesus. We are his lifeblood.
We understand God is a Spirit; he does not need blood to
be. He is the "I Am," the self-existing one. In this sense,
the blood is the lowest denominator of life, a means of
expressing, maintaining, and holding life in us. What else
could be more precious, more powerful, and more fully an
expression of God's love than allowing the sacrifice of his
only begotten Son for our sins? He did this so that his decree
that the wages of sin were death was met.

Our lives are the bloodline and byproduct of that
sacrifice. We are covered by the anointing of Jesus' sacrifice
for our sins. What it must have felt like to take on the burden

of sin for the whole world and the inherent stench and foul rottenness of the evil that came with it. O' how high was the price that was paid! No amount of money could compensate for that; only the blood of Jesus was the qualified medium of exchange.

Jesus became the living Holy of Holies, a covering for us. Hebrews 10:12 testifies, "But this man, after he had offered one sacrifice for sins for ever, sat down on the right hand of God." The mercy seat was where God met with man. God said in Exodus 25:22, "And there I will meet with thee, and I will commune with thee from above the mercy seat." The mercy seat was the lid of the Ark of the Covenant that at one time contained the presence or glory of God.

> The original Hebrew word translated as Mercy Seat, is the Hebrew word Kap-po-reth, and means to cover in two ways; as a noun, meaning a lid or a top, but also based on the Hebrew root from which it was derived, as a verb meaning to pardon, or to atone for, as in to cover a debt. (Blank n.d.)

I like this definition because it fits the role of Jesus in becoming the sacrifice for sins of the world. He indeed paid the debt by his lifeblood. Our sins were atoned for and pardoned.

Exodus 26:34 testifies, "And thou shalt put the mercy seat upon the ark of the testimony in the most holy place."

The high priest was the only person permitted to enter the most holy place where the mercy seat was on the Day of Atonement with the blood sacrifice that was sprinkled on the mercy seat. By the time of the New Testament, the symbolic meaning and purpose of the mercy seat was made clear—Jesus, the most high priest appearing before the throne of God in heaven after making atonement for all sin.

We can be certain that we are covered by the Blood of Jesus. There should be no doubt whatsoever that his blood saved us. Its power remains on earth as it is in heaven forever pleading our case before God. If you need another Scripture witness, read Hebrews 9:24: "For Christ is not entered into the holy places made with hands, which are the figures of the true; but into heaven itself, now to appear in the presence of God for us." The holy places were the Holy Place and Holy of Holies that was built according to God's express design as a temporary satisfaction, a foreshadowing of Jesus. However, Jesus did not go there; he went to heaven. He is now the Holy of Holies, and the covering of the Ark of the Covenant, our mercy seat as there is no longer a need for a place built by man's hands. God gave Moses instructions on how to build the Holy of Holies. This was a temporary set-up and another splendid example of God's architectural detail.

To understand the covering, we must realize the significance of the Ark of the Covenant. Leviticus 16:15–17 tells us,

Then shall he kill the goat of the sin offering, that is for the people, and bring his blood within the veil, and do with that blood as he did with the blood of the bullock, and sprinkle it upon the mercy seat, and before the mercy seat: And he shall make an atonement for the holy place, because of the uncleanness of the children of Israel, and because of their transgressions in all their sins: and so shall he do for the tabernacle of the congregation, that remaineth among them in the midst of their uncleanness. And there shall be no man in the tabernacle of the congregation when he goeth in to make an atonement in the holy place, until he come out, and have made an atonement for himself, and for his household, and for all the congregation of Israel.

Our Scripture witness 1 John 1:1, 14 testifies,

In the beginning was the Word, and the Word was with God, and the Word was God ... And the Word was made flesh, and dwelt among us, (and we beheld his glory, the glory as of the only begotten of the Father,) full of grace and truth.

The first blood sacrifices and the mercy seat were symbols or types of the blood sacrifice and covering of Jesus for our sins. Our Scripture witness Hebrews 9:12 testifies, "Neither by the blood of goats and calves, but by his own blood he entered in once into the Holy Place, having obtained eternal redemption for us." The blood of Jesus gives us access to the magnificence of God's glory. It was in the Ark of the Covenant until Jesus accomplished his task and would once again become the Holy of Holies.

John 17:4–5 testifies that Jesus was praying to God the Father, "I have glorified thee on the earth: I have finished the work which thou gavest me to do. And now, O Father, glorify thou me with thine own self with the glory which I had with thee before the world was." John 14:6 testifies, "Jesus saith unto him, I am the way [meaning the access to God], the truth [meaning the Word], and the life [meaning life and eternal life]: no man cometh unto the Father, but by me."

The Scripture explains itself with co-witnesses as the Bible will always bear witness Scripture to Scripture. Our Scripture witnesses 1 Timothy 2:5–6 testifies, "For there is one God, and one mediator between God and men, the man Jesus Christ Who gave himself a ransom for all." In 1 John 1:2, which further defines Jesus' position as a blood cover, we read, "For the life was manifested, and we have seen it, and bear witness, and shew unto you that eternal life, which was with the Father, and was manifested unto us." I believe Scripture will always explain and reveal itself with a Scripture witness. Another witness is 1 John 3:8, which testifies to the others, "For this purpose the Son of God was manifested, that he might destroy the works of the devil." Jesus' death on the cross was foreordained by him. Our Scripture witness John 1:1–3 testifies,

> In the beginning was the Word, and the Word was with God, and the Word was God. The same was in the beginning with God. All things were made by him; and without him was not anything made that was made.

Jesus, our mercy seat, communes with God as our intercessor, mediator, and advocate. He also made the way for us to come boldly to the throne and make our request known to God. Jesus' blood sacrifice was a divine work of the Holy Trinity, the Godhead.

We can take comfort in this supreme demonstration of unconditional love and glory in the blood cover provided by this atoning act of Jesus, which is not a mere covering but a saturation of the knowledge and power of his sacrifice. Saturation means "to cause to be thoroughly soaked, imbued or penetrated; and to cause something to be filled, charged, supplied, etc. with the maximum that can be absorbed" (Webster's New World, 2010). Once our hearts and spirits become saturated with the knowledge of the blood sacrifice of Jesus, we enter into a new dimension of faith and power sustained by the Word of God. The knowledge of the Word is not complete without knowledge of the power of the blood sacrifice of Jesus. "Be covered to become saturated". You might be surprised to find out which drops of blood Jesus personally and individually shed for your sin. Our Scripture witness Deuteronomy 33:12 testifies, "The beloved of the LORD shall dwell in safety by him; and the Lord shall cover him all the day long, and he shall dwell between his shoulders."

Revelation 1:5 testifies, "Unto him that loved us, and washed us from our sins **in his own blood.**" (Emphasis added) If blood did not have a major significance to God, why would he have prepared Jesus a body with blood? The Word became the blood of eternal life.

Jesus deserves the highest praise, the most profound worship, and the total and absolute devotion of our lives to him; to hold back anything from him is sacrilege. Jesus did it all, and all he did should not be for nothing; as Hebrew 6:6 testifies, "If they shall fall away, to renew them again unto repentance; seeing they crucify to themselves the Son of God afresh, and put him to an open shame [again]." We have been bought with an exceedingly high price; we are obligated to give him our life in return as a living sacrifice. We can only be blessed because we are already covered by the blood.

As I was writing, the Holy Spirit continually "urged" me to "go deeper." Blood is an extremely personal issue, just as it was personal for Jesus to die for our sins. We have only scratched the surface in this book. Even though the knowledge of the power of the blood sacrifice of Jesus is unfathomable and unlimited, we have a sacred responsibility to go deeper. The deeper we go, the more revelation we will find. We will become so saturated that we will not able to tell where the blood leaves off and we begin. A simpler way to say this is go deep enough to satisfy Jesus!

I strongly encourage you to dedicate yourself to increasing your knowledge of the blood by continuing your study. Use the study guide and workbook integrator that follows up this book as a teaching tool, it will challenge you to "Go deeper". You will go beyond this surface study and into the depth of the cover of the blood of Jesus. **Then** I challenge you to go even deeper, just as the Holy Spirit challenged me!

I'm covered by the blood. Are you?

CHAPTER 12

SCRIPTURES FOR MEDITATION

In 1 John 2:27, we read,

> But the anointing which ye have received of
> him abideth in you, and ye need not that any
> man teach you: but as the same anointing
> teacheth you of all things, and is truth, and is
> no lie, and even as it hath taught you, ye shall
> abide in him.

The understanding and revelation of the subject of
the blood of Christ requires deep mediation of the Word
concerning the blood of Christ. According to *Webster's
New World Dictionary*, meditation means "deep reflection,
especially in sacred matters; oral or written material as
a sermon, based on meditation" (Guralnik 1982). The
dictionary also provides that meditate means "to study;
ponder; to think deeply and continuously; reflect" (Guralnik

1982). As these definitions clearly indicate, this is deep reflection and deep thought focused on sacred matters, in this case, the blood of Jesus. Studying the blood of Jesus will bring the subject to light in your own life; the more you meditate on it, the more it will become a part of your psyche— your soul. We understand that this is our mind, will, and emotions. However, meditation also brings the entire tripod of the man into a deeper revelation of God's intent and Jesus' fulfillment in his blood sacrifice. This knowledge gained through meditating the Word becomes embedded in us. We cannot be separate from how God created us in his image.

Meditating the Word regarding the blood sacrifice of Jesus is a melting together of our faith in the blood and its power. The more we meditate on the blood of Jesus, the more we become familiar with his power and his divine position in our lives. Nothing meditated on continually will be forgotten, and As a matter of fact, meditating on the blood should be an essential part of our worship. Remember, "Go deeper!" Meditation takes us deeper; it is the way to remain in constant, close contact with the power. Meditation on the blood sacrifice of Jesus should be a sacred time of one-to-one communion with Jesus Christ. You will find yourself caught up in the revelation and peace of being with him on another level in his blood. Meditation will also help you recollect yourself, refocus, and prioritize how and where the blood will takes its place in your life. The blood was not shed just to fall on the ground but to fall into our hearts and spirits—alive and continuously bringing forth new revelation.

Meditation is not just a thinking process, because the blood of Christ goes beyond mental processes. It is a deep reflection on a sacred matter. It connects our soul to the divinity of Jesus and the divine qualities and attributes of all the names and titles of Jesus. By this, you are connected to the power and abilities his names and titles hold.

It is extremely important to set aside meditation time devoted to specifically on meditating on the blood of Jesus. Here is a way to meditate.

1. Set aside a specific time.
2. Shut out distractions.
3. Set aside a specific place.
4. Gather the Scriptures for meditation.
5. Remember that anytime you honor the blood that three things may occur:
   a. immediate presence of the Holy Spirit
   b. distractions and disturbances
   c. attempted attacks by the enemy

Our Scripture witnesses are as follows.

- Psalm 19:14, testifies "Let the words of my mouth, and the meditation of my heart, be acceptable in thy sight, O LORD, my strength, and my redeemer."

- Joshua 1:8: "This book of the law shall not depart out of thy mouth; but thou shalt meditate therein day and night, that thou mayest observe to do according to all that is written therein: for then thou shalt make thy way prosperous, and then thou shalt have good success."
- Psalm 1:2: "But his delight is in the law of the LORD; and in his law doth he meditate day and night."

As I have repeatedly said, The Bible always explains itself with Scriptures that witness for or to each other. The prophets as oracles of God foretold events to prove God's divine actions.

The Word did its job, and the prophets did theirs. Our job is to after having heard the Word, develop our faith in it and meditate on it until it becomes a lifestyle. The more we are in the Word, the more the Word will be revealed to us.

It is very important to continue to peruse, study, and meditate the Scriptures related to the blood sacrifice of Jesus Christ. We are responsible for our own growth and maturity in the knowledge base that we acquire. We believe things from our own understanding and comprehension much more strongly when have learned the truth of them for ourselves.

Do not merely accept what you have read; know it for yourself, and allow the Holy Spirit, the consummate teacher, to guide and teach you.

Below are Scriptures on the subject of blood of Jesus, a concept woven throughout the Bible. They will be a good point of reference to begin a meditation session. There is blood everywhere.

Meditation Scripture on the Blood of Jesus

Matthew 3:16–17: "And Jesus, when he was baptized, went up straightway out of the water: and, lo, the heavens were opened unto him, and he saw the Spirit of God descending like a dove, and lighting upon him: And lo a voice from heaven, saying, This is my beloved Son, in whom I am well pleased."

Matthew 26:28: "For this is my blood of the new testament, which is shed for many for the remission of sins."

Luke 22:42: "Father, if thou be willing, remove this cup from me: nevertheless not my will, but thine, be done."

Romans 5:8–12: "But God commendeth his love toward us, in that, while we were yet sinners, Christ died for us. Much more then, being now justified by his blood, we shall be saved from wrath through him. For if, when we were enemies, we were reconciled to God by the death of his Son, much more, being reconciled, we shall be saved by his life. And not only so, but we also joy in God through our Lord Jesus Christ, by whom we have now received the atonement. Wherefore, as by one man sin entered into the world, and death by sin; and so death passed upon all men, for that all have sinned."

Romans 3:23–25: "For all have sinned, and come short of the glory of God; Being justified freely by his grace through the redemption that is in Christ Jesus: Whom God hath set forth to be a propitiation through faith in his blood, to declare his righteousness for the remission of sins that are past, through the forbearance of God."

1 Corinthians 10:16: "The cup of blessing which we bless, is it not the communion of the blood of Christ? The bread which we break, is it not the communion of the body of Christ?"

Ephesians 1:7: "In whom we redemption through his blood, the forgiveness for sins, according to the riches of his grace."

Ephesians 2:13–16: "But now in Christ Jesus ye who sometimes were far off are made nigh by the blood of Christ. For he is our peace, who hath made both one, and hath broken down the middle wall of partition between us; Having abolished in his flesh the enmity, even the law of commandments contained in ordinances; for to make in himself of twain one new man, so making peace; And that he might reconcile both unto God in one body by the cross, having slain the enmity thereby."

Colossians 1:13–14: " Who hath delivered us from the power of darkness, and hath translated us into the kingdom of his dear Son: In whom we have redemption through his blood, even the forgiveness of sins."

Colossians 1:20: "And having made peace through the blood of this cross, by him to reconcile all things unto himself: by him, I say, whether they be things in earth, or things in heaven."

Hebrews 1:2–3 "[God] Hath in these last days spoken unto us by his Son, whom he hath appointed heir of all things, by whom also he made the worlds; Who being the brightness of his glory, and the express image of his person, and upholding all things by the word of his power, when he had by himself purged our sins, sat down on the right hand of the Majesty on high."

Hebrews 2:9: "But we see Jesus, who was made a little lower than the angels for the suffering of death, crowned with glory and honor; that he by the grace of God should taste death for every man."

Hebrews 2:14: "Forasmuch then as the children are partakers of flesh and blood, he also likewise took part of the same; that through death he might destroy him that had the power of death, that is, the devil."

Hebrews 2:16: "For verily he took not on him the nature of angels; but he took on him the seed of Abraham."

Hebrews 7:26–27: "For such an high priest became us, who is holy, harmless, undefiled, separate from sinners, and made higher than the heavens; Who needeth not daily, as those high priests, to offer up sacrifice, first for his own sins, and then for the people's: for this he did once, when he offered up himself."

Hebrews 8:6, 13: "But now hath he obtained a more excellent ministry, by how much also he is the mediator of a better covenant, which was established upon better promises ... In that he saith, A new covenant, he hath made the first old. Now that which decayeth and waxeth old is ready to vanish away."

Hebrews 9:7: "But into the second went the high priest alone once every year, not without blood, which he offered for himself, and for the errors of the people."

Hebrews 9:11–14 "But Christ being come an high priest of good things to come, by a greater and more perfect tabernacle, not made with hands, that is to say, not of this building; Neither by the blood of goats and calves, but by his own blood he entered in once into the holy place, having obtained eternal redemption for us. For if the blood of bulls and of goats, and the ashes of an heifer sprinkling the unclean, sanctifieth to the purifying of the flesh: How much more shall the blood of Christ, who through the eternal Spirit offered himself without spot to God, purge your conscience from dead works to serve the living God?"

Hebrews 10:19–20 "Having therefore, brethren, boldness to enter into the holiest by the blood of Jesus, By a new and living way, which he hath consecrated for us, through the veil, that is to say, his flesh."

Hebrews 12:2: "Looking unto Jesus the author and finisher of our faith; who for the joy that was set before him endured the cross, despising the shame, and is set down at the right hand of God."

Hebrews 12:4: "Ye have not yet resisted unto blood, striving against sin."

Hebrews 13:20: "Now the God of peace, that brought again from the dead our Lord Jesus, that great shepherd of the sheep, through the blood of the everlasting covenant."

1 Peter 1:2: "Elect according to the foreknowledge of God the Father, through sanctification of the Spirit, unto obedience and sprinkling of the blood of Jesus Christ: Grace unto you, and peace, be multiplied."

1 Peter 1:18–21 "Forasmuch as ye know that ye were not redeemed with corruptible things, as silver and gold, from your vain conversation received by tradition from your fathers; But with the precious blood of Christ, as of a lamb without blemish and without spot: Who verily was foreordained before the foundation of the world, but was manifest in these last times for you, Who by him do believe in God, that raised him up from the dead, and gave him glory; that your faith and hope might be in God."

1 John 2:2: "And he is the propitiation for our sins: and not for ours only, but also for the sins of the whole world."

1 John 3:8: "He that committeth sin is of the devil; for the devil sinneth from the beginning. For this purpose the Son of God was manifested, that he might destroy the works of the devil."

1 John 5:6: "This is he that came by water and blood, even Jesus Christ; not by water only, but by water and blood. And it is the Spirit that beareth witness, because the Spirit is truth."

Revelation 1:5–6 "And from Jesus Christ, who is the faithful witness, and the first begotten of the dead, and the prince of the kings of the earth. Unto him that loved us, and washed us from our sins in his blood, And hath made us kings and priests unto God and his Father; to him be glory and dominion forever and ever. Amen."

Revelation 5:12: "Saying with a loud voice, Worthy is the Lamb that was slain to receive power, and riches, and wisdom, and strength, and honor, and glory, and blessing."

Revelation 7:13–14 "And one of the elders, answered, saying unto me, What are these which are arrayed in white robes? And whence came they? And I said unto him, Sir, thou knowest. And he said to me, These are they which came out of great tribulation, and have washed their robes, and made them white in the blood of the Lamb."

Revelation 12:11: "And they overcame him by the blood of the lamb, and by the word of their testimony."

Blood Songs

Songs of worship and praise are a dedication to and communication with God. Music is a universal experience. I believe every living creature is moved or affected by music and sounds of worship. Even our scripture witness, Luke 19:37-40, clearly expresses this thought.

37 And when he was come nigh, even now at the descent of the mount of Olives, the whole multitude of the disciples began to rejoice and praise God with a loud voice for all the mighty works that they had seen;

38 Saying, Blessed be the King that cometh in the name of the Lord: peace in heaven, and glory in the highest.

39 And some of the Pharisees from among the multitude said unto him, Master, rebuke thy disciples.

40 And he answered and said unto them, I tell you that, if these should hold their peace, the stones would immediately cry out.

Those that give glory and honor to the blood sacrifice of Jesus are especially anointed and powerful. The Bible often speaks of worship and praise. Psalms is described as the inspired prayer and praise book of Israel. Many praise songs have come directly from these Scriptures.

Blood songs, however, are borne out of and come from the inward witness of the knowledge of the blood sacrifice of Jesus. The power of the blood is in them and on them and is poured out of them like the "healing balm." True worship has a way of taking you someplace with God, not only to him, but with Him. Our Scripture witness John 4:23–24 testifies,

> But the hour cometh, and now is, when the
> true worshippers shall worship the Father in
> spirit and in truth: for the Father seeketh such
> to worship him. God is a Spirit: and they that
> worship him must worship him in spirit and
> in truth.

Blood songs have a divine ability to usher in the presence of the Holy Spirit. For whenever the blood of Jesus is acknowledged, the Holy Spirit will manifest himself. Once the Holy Spirit is manifested, he will demonstrate all his attributes in full effect. There is nothing like exposing the rarefied holiness of the blood and its power to heal, comfort, and save.

I believe revival will be once again ushered in when we go back to worshiping God as true worshipers. We will hold up the "Blood stained banner" as spoken of in our old time religious services. The renewed focus on the knowledge of the blood sacrifice of Jesus will be the heralding of next "Azusa Street" style revival. The blood sacrifice of Jesus, the blood that changed the world—shout about it, dance, and sing about it. Praise God for it!

"Nothing but the Blood"

What can wash away my sin?
Nothing but the blood of Jesus;
What can make me whole again?
Nothing but the blood of Jesus.

Refrain
Oh! precious is the flow
That makes me white as snow;
No other fount I know,
Nothing but the blood of Jesus.

Refrain
For my pardon, this I see,
Nothing but the blood of Jesus;
For my cleansing this my plea,
Nothing but the blood of Jesus.

Refrain
Nothing can for sin atone,
Nothing but the blood of Jesus;
Naught of good that I have done,
Nothing but the blood of Jesus.

Refrain
This is all my hope and peace,
Noting but the blood of Jesus;

This is all my righteousness,
Nothing but the blood of Jesus.

Refrain
Now by this I'll overcome—
Nothing but the blood of Jesus,
Now by this I'll reach my home—
Nothing but the blood of Jesus.

Refrain
Glory! Glory! This I sing—
Nothing but the blood of Jesus,
All my praise for this I bring—
Nothing but the blood of Jesus.

—Words and Music: Robert Lowry, in Gospel Music, by William Doane and Robert Lowry, New York: Biglow and Main, 1876.

"Covered by the Blood"

Section A

I'm covered by the blood. I'm covered by the blood
From the garden in agony to the nailing to
the tree, the blood of Jesus covered me.
Out of God's great grace, love and
mercy Jesus died just for me.
I am covered by His blood.
I am covered by His blood.
Covered with healing.
Covered with protection.
Covered with power.

Section B

From the garden in agony to the nailing to
the tree, the blood of Jesus covered me.
How we are covered is how we overcame
by the blood of the lamb,
So I plead a cover of healing
I plead a cover of protection over me.
I am covered by His blood.
I am covered by His blood.

Section C

From the garden in agony to the nailing to
the tree, the blood of Jesus covered me.

His blood a living perfection with the
same power of His resurrection.
I am covered by the blood.
I am covered by the blood. I am covered by the blood.

— Rita Y. Jarrett

"Calvary"

Refrain
Calvary, Calvary, Calvary
Calvary, Calvary, Calvary
Surely He died on Calvary.

Verse 1
Ev'ry time I think about Jesus,
Ev'ry time I think about Jesus,
Ev'ry time I think about Jesus

Verse 2
Sinner, do you love my Jesus?
Sinner, do you love my Jesus?
Sinner, do you love my Jesus?

Verse 3
We are climbing Jacob's ladder,
We are climbing Jacob's ladder,
We are climbing Jacob's ladder,
Surely He died on Calvary.

Verse 4
Ev'ry round goes higher and higher,
Ev'ry round goes higher and higher,
Ev'ry round goes higher and higher.

— African American Heritage Hymnal. 2001 (c) GIA Publications, Luke 23:33.

"The Blood Will Never Lose Its Power"

Verse

The blood that Jesus shed for me
Way back on Calvary
The blood that gives me strength from day to day
It will never lose its pow'r
It reaches form the highest mountain (mountain)
And it flows to the lowest valley (valley)
The blood that gives me strength from day to day
It will never lose its pow'r

—African American Heritage Hymnal. 2001. (c) GIA
Publications, Romans 5:9.

"There is Power in the Blood"

Verse 1

Would you be free from the burden of sin?
There's pow'r in the blood, pow'r in the blood
Would you o'er evil a victory win?
There is wonderful pow'r in the blood
There is pow'r, pow'r, wonderful working pow'r
In the blood of the Lamb
There is pow'r, pow'r, wonderful working pow'r
In the precious blood of the Lamb.

Verse 2

Would you be free from your passion and pride?
There's pow'r in the blood, pow'r in the blood
Come for a cleansing to Calvary's tide
There is wonderful pow'r in the blood
There is pow'r, pow'r, wonderful working pow'r
In the blood of the Lamb
There is pow'r, pow'r, wonderful working pow'r
In the precious blood of the Lamb.

Verse 3

Would you be whiter, yes brighter than snow
There's pow'r in the blood, pow'r in the blood
Sin stains are lost in its life-giving flow
There is wonderful pow'r in the blood
There is pow'r, pow'r, wonderful working pow'r

In the blood of the Lamb
There is pow'r, pow'r, wonderful working pow'r
In the precious blood of the Lamb.

Verse 4

Would you do service for Jesus, your King?
There's pow'r in the blood, pow'r in the blood
Would you live daily His praises to sing?
There is wonderful pow'r in the blood
There is pow'r, pow'r, wonderful working pow'r
In the blood of the Lamb
There is pow'r, pow'r, wonderful working pow'r
In the precious blood of the Lamb.

—African American Heritage Hymnal. 2001. (c) GIA Publications.

"Nothing But the Blood of Jesus"

Verse 1

What can wash away my sin?
Nothing but the blood of Jesus
What can make me whole again?
Nothing but the blood of Jesus
Oh! precious is the flow
That makes me white as snow
No other fount I know
Nothing but the blood of Jesus

Verse 2

For my pardon this I see
Nothing but the blood of Jesus
For my cleansing, this my plea
Nothing but the blood of Jesus
Oh! precious is the flow
That makes me white as snow
No other fount I know
Nothing but the blood of Jesus

Verse 3

Nothing can for sin atone
Nothing but the blood of Jesus
Naught of good that I have done
Nothing but the blood of Jesus
Oh! precious is the flow

That makes me white as snow
No other fount I know
Nothing but the blood of Jesus

Verse 4
This is all my hope and peace
Nothing but the blood of Jesus
This is all my righteousness
Nothing but the blood of Jesus
Oh! precious is the flow
That makes me white as snow
No other fount I know
Nothing but the blood of Jesus

—African American Heritage Hymnal. 2001. (c) GIA Publications, Hebrew 9:22.

"Alas! And Did My Savior Bleed"

Verse 1

Alas! And did my Savior bleed
And did my Sov'reign die?
Would He devote that sacred head
For sinners such as I?

Verse 2

Was it for crimes that I have done
He groaned up on the tree?
Amazing pity! Grace unknown!
And love beyond degree!

Verse 3

Well might the sun in darkness hide
And shut His glories in
When God, the mighty maker died
For man that the creature's sin

Verse 4

But drops of grief can ne'er repay
The debt of love I owe
Here, Lord, I give myself away
'Tis all that I can do

—African American Heritage Hymnal. 2001. (c) GIA Publications, Romans 5:8.

"Oh, The Blood of Jesus"

Verse 1

Oh, the blood of Jesus
Oh, the blood of Jesus
Oh, the blood of Jesus
It must not suffer loss—loss
Wonder-working pow'r
In the blood, the blood, of the Lamb
of the Lamb
There is power, power, power, power
Wonder-working pow'r
In the precious blood of the Lamb

Verse 2

Oh, the word of Jesus
Oh, the word of Jesus
Oh, the word of Jesus
it cleanses white as snow—snow
There is power, power, power
Wonder-working pow'r
In the blood, the blood, of the Lamb
of the Lamb
There is power, power, power, power
Wonder-working pow'r
In the precious blood of the Lamb

Verse 3

Oh, the love of Jesus

Oh, the love of Jesus

Oh, the love of Jesus

It makes His body whole—whole

There is power, power, power, power

Wonder-working pow'r

In the blood, the blood, of the Lamb

of the Lamb

There is power, power, power, power

Wonder-working pow'r

In the precious blood of the Lamb

—African American Heritage Hymnal. 2001. (c) GIA Publications, 1 Peter 1:18–19.

"I Know It Was the Blood"

Verse 1
I know it was the blood,
I know it was the blood
I know it was the blood for me
One day when I was lost He died upon the cross
I know it was the blood for me

Verse 2
They whipped Him all night long
They whipped Him all night long
They whipped Him all night long for me
One day when I was lost He died upon the cross
I know it was the blood for me

Verse 3
They pierced Him in His side
They pierced Him in His side
They pierced Him in His side for me
One day when I was lost He died upon the cross
I know it was the blood for me

Verse 4
He never said a mumblin' word
He never said a mumblin' word
He never said a mumblin' word for me
One day when I was lost He died upon the cross
I know it was the blood for me

Verse 5

He hung His head and died

He hung His head and died

He hung His head and died for me

One day when I was lost He died upon the cross

I know it was the blood for me

Verse 6

He's coming back again

He's coming back again

He's coming back again for me

One day when I was lost He died upon the cross

I know it was the blood for me

—African American Heritage Hymnal. 2001. (c) GIA Publications, Ephesians 1:7–8.

A Synopsis of the Blood of Jesus

A brief general review, condensation, summary supported by Scripture witnesses.

What Jesus Did and Why

1. **It was foreordained before the foundation of the world.**
   1 John 1:1–3
   1 Peter 1:20
2. **Born of a woman who conceived a body prepared by God and assisted by the Holy Spirit.**
   Genesis 3:15
   Matthew 2:21
   Luke 1:27–32
3. **Became flesh and blood.**
   John 1:14
   Hebrews 2:14, 16
4. **Left his position with the Father in heaven.**
   John 17:5, 24
   John 16:28
5. **Preached, taught, and healed and had an earthly ministry.**
   Matthew 4:17
   Matthew 4:23
   1 John 3:8

6. **Became a living sacrifice as the Lamb of God.**

   John 1:29, 36

   1 Peter 1:19

   Revelation 5:12

7. **Walked and lived among us in the world.**

   John 1:14

8. **Was touched by our infirmities.**

   Hebrews 4:15

   Matthews 8:17

   Romans 8:26

9. **Was tempted.**

   Hebrews 4:15

   Hebrews 2:18

10. **Suffered.**

    Hebrews 2:9

    Hebrews 5:8

    Hebrews 9:26

    Hebrews 13:12

    1 Peter 2:21

    1 Peter 3:18

    1 Peter 4:1

    Romans 6:5

    Matthew 16:21

    2 Timothy 2:12

11. **Provided a better covenant established upon better promises.**

    Hebrews 8:6

12. **Endured the cross and was crucified.**

    Luke 23:26

    John 19:17

    Ephesians 2:16

    Philippians 2:8

13. **Died for our sins and the sins of the world.**

    Matthew 26:28

    Luke 11:14

    Acts 23:38

    Romans 11:27

14. **Went to hell and was resurrected back to life.**

    John 11:25

    Acts 1:22

    I Peter 1:3

    Philippians 3:10

15. **Became an intercessor.**

    Romans 8:27

    Romans 8:34

    Romans 11:2

16. **Defeated satan, death, and hell.**

    Revelation 1:18

17. **Upheld the world by this word.**

    Hebrews 1:3

18. **Loves us.**

    John 13:34

    John 15:9

    John 16:29

19. **Shed his blood.**

 Matthew 23:35

 Matthew 26:26

 Luke 11:50

 Luke 22:20

20. **Became the hypostatic union.**

 Matthew 3:16–17

 Matthew 12:8

 Matthew 8:29

 Matthew 10:23

 Matthew 2:28

Rationale as to Why Jesus Did It

1. **To fulfill the Scriptures and the foreordained plan of God.**

 John 13:18

 John 17:12

 John 15:25

 Luke 4:21

 Matthew 26:54

 Matthew 24:34

 Matthew 14:49

 Leviticus 20:3

2. **Because He loves us.**

 Romans 8:35

 2 Corinthians 5:14

 John 3:16

3. **For our salvation.**
   Hebrews 1:4
   Jonah 2:9
   Romans 1:16
   Revelation 7:10

4. **Redemption and reconciliation.**
   Isaiah 49:26
   Romans 3:24
   Ephesians 1:7
   2 Corinthians 5:18
   2 Corinthians 5:19

5. **Our Healing.**
   1 Peter 2:24
   Luke 4:18

6. **Eternal Life.**
   John 6:54
   John 10:28
   John 17:2
   John 17:3
   2 Timothy 6:19
   Hebrews 5:9
   I John 2:25
   Jude 21

7. **Atonement.**
   Exodus 30:10
   Exodus 30:16
   Romans 5:11
   2 Samuel 21:3

8. **Our Peace.**
   John 14:27
   Ephesians 2:14
   1 Corinthians 7:15
   Isaiah 9:6

9. **Our Hope.**
   1 Corinthians 9:10
   1 Timothy 1:1
   Titus 2:13
   Hebrews 6:11

10. **Joy.**
    Nehemiah 8:10
    Romans 14:17

11. **Sent the Holy Spirit, our comforter.**
    John 14:16
    John 14:26
    John 15:26
    John 16:7

12. **Defeated and destroyed the devil.**
    1 John 3:8

13. **Our deliverer.**
    Matthew 11:27
    Acts 7:10
    Colossians 1:13
    2 Corinthians 1:10
    1 Timothy 3:11

Who Jesus Did It For

1. Me
2. You
3. The World (1 John 2:2)

REFERENCES

American Society of Hematology. (2013). Blood basics. Retrieved from www.Hematology.org/patients/blood-basics/5222. aspx

Bennett, D. (2011). *Three coins.* Retrieved from books. google.com/books?id=5OPs6CNu76sC&printsec=fr ontcover&dq=three+coins&hl=en&sa=X&ei=ZewE U5b-KqOdyQGW7YGgCA&ved=0CCsQ6AEwAA#v =onepage&q=three%20coin&f=false

Bible, L. (2006). *Finis Jennings Dake: His Life and Ministry.* Retrieved from luke418min.com/page2.html

Bible, L. (1998). *Theological Summary of the Writings of "Finis Jennings Dake."* Retrieved from www.dakebible.com/WebPages/ dake-theology.htm

Bickle, B. and S. Jantz. (1999). *Knowing God 101.* Eugene, Ore.: Harvard House.

Blank, W. (n.d.). "To cover." Retrieved from www.keyway.ca/ htm2005/20050305.htm

"Blood facts." (2007). Retrieved from www.bloodindex.org/ blood_facts.php

"Blood type facts." (2013). Retrieved from www.bloodbook. com/type-facts.html

"Bone Marrow." (2014). Retrieved from medical-dictionary. thefreedictionary.com/bone+marrow

Booker, R. (2009). *Celebrating Jesus in the biblical feasts.* Shippensburg, Pa.: Destiny Image Publishers.

Choen-Regev, S. (2012). Learn Hebrew online topic: tu bishvat. *Jerusalem Post.* Retrieved from www.jpost.com/ promocontent/learning-Hebrew-online

Cocherell, B. L. (2008, February 10). "The beard law: insult and humiliation." Retrieved from www.bibleresearch.org/ articles/alw5.htm

Copeland, K. (1995). *John G. Lake: His Life, His Sermons, His Boldness of Faith.* Fort Worth: Kenneth Copeland.

"The crucifixion: these last days tract 13f—supplement to Lesson 13." (n.d.). Retrieved from www.pathlights.com/ theselastdays/tracts/tract_13f.htm

Dainty, C. (n.d.). "Haematology in clinical practice: clinical practice 4." Retrieved from www.sthk.nhs.uk/library/ documents/haematologyhandbook.pdf

Dake, F. J. (1996). *Dake's Annotated Reference Bible.* Lawrenceville, Ga.: Dake Publishing.

DiGiovanna, A. G. (1994). "Respiratory system. *Human aging: biological perspective.*" (Chapter 5, PDF). Retrieved from www2.ku.edu/~lba/courses/articles/chapter%205d.pdf

Dodd, S. R. (2001). "ABC of vascular disease: arterial haemodynamics." Retrieved from www.simondodds.com/ Arterial/Occlusive/Haemodynamics/Haemodynamics.htm

Eby, J. P. (n.d.). "In end time revelation the royal priesthood, Part 29: the Melchizedek connection." Retrieved from www. sigler.org/eby/priest29.html

Fry, B. (2003, November 11). *Chromosomes, somatids, and the blood of Christ.* Retrieved from www.anchorstone.com/content/index.php?option=com_content&task=view&id=135&Itemid=55

Gigot, F. (1907). "The bosom of Abraham." In *The Catholic Encyclopedia.* Retrieved from www.newadvent.org/cathen/01055a.htm

Houdmann, S. M. (2008). "What is the Via Dolorosa?" Retrieved from wwwgotquestions.org/Via-Dolorosa.html

Guralnik, D. B., ed. (1982). *Webster's New World Dictionary* (second concise ed.). New York: Simon and Schuster

Halley, H. H. (1962). *Halley's Bible Handbook* (twenty-third edition). Grand Rapids, Mi.: Zondervan.

Hinn, B. (1993). *The Blood: Its Power from Genesis to Jesus to You.* Lake Mary, Fl.: Creation House.

Holmes, P. (2013, April 19). Christianity: blood, blood and more blood. Retrieved from www.raanetwork.org/christianity-blood-blood-and-more-blood

"How he died: a medical/forensic look at the crucifixion of Jesus." (2006). Retrieved from crucifixionshroud-com.htm

"Jesus' nails—what do we know about nails?" (2002). Retrieved from www.allaboutjesuschrist.org/jesus-nails-faq.htm

"Beard." (2008). In *Jewish Encyclopedia Online.* Retrieved from www.jewishencyclopedia.com/articles/2690-beard

"Eve." (2011). In *Jewish Encyclopedia Online.* Retrieved from www.jewishencyclopedia.com/articles/5916-eve

"Flogging." (2008). In *Jewish Virtual Library.* Retrieved from www.jewishvirtuallibrary.org/jsource/judaica/ejud_0002_0007_0_06574.html

Keller, W. (1956). *The Bible As History*. New York: William Morrow.

Lambrianides, A. (n.d.). "The cross of Christ." Retrieved from www.scionofzion.com/cross_of_christ.htm

Lamm, M. (n.d.). "Modesty (Tz'ni'ut): discretion in appearance and speech is designed to protect our souls from assault by a coarse world." Retrieved from www.myjewishlearning.com/practices/Ethics/Our_Bodies/Clothing/Modesty.shtml

"Materiam Superabat Opus" (def. 1). (2008). In *Latin-Dictionary online*. Retrieved from www.latin-dictionary.org/Materiam_superabat_opus

Luckmann, J. K. C. Sorensen. (1974). *Medical-Surgical Nursing*. Philadelphia: W. B. Saunders.

Meacham, J. (2009, April 4). The end of Christian America. Newsweek. Retrieved from http://www.newsweek.com/2009/04/03/the-end-of-christian-america.print.html -

Melton, J. G. (1984). The vampire book: the encyclopedia of the undead. Detroit, MI: Visible Ink Press.

Murray, A. (1993). *The Power of the Blood of Jesus*. New Kensington, Pa.: Whitaker House.

National Geographic. (2013). "Lungs." *National Geographic online*. Retrieved from science.nationalgeographic.com/science/health-and-human-body/human-body/lungs-article/?rptregcta=reg_free_np&rptregcampaign=20131016_rw_membership_r1p_us_se_w#close-modal

"Chayah" (def. 1). (2013). In *Old Testament Hebrew Lexicon—New American Standard Online*. Retrieved from www.biblestudytools.com/lexicons/hebrew/nas/chayah.html

"Kaphar" (def. 1). (2013). In *Old Testament Hebrew Lexicon—New American Standard Online*. Retrieved from www.biblestudytools.com/search/?q=atonement&rc=LEX&rc2=LEX+HEB&ps=10&s=References

"The human body is about two-thirds oxygen: oxygen's influence and its role in human body." (n.d.). Retrieved from www.oxygen-review.com/human-body.html

OpenStax College. (2013, June 19). *Anatomy and Physiology*. Retrieved from cnx.org/content/col11496/1.6/

Pace, E. (1910). "Hypostatic Union." In *The Catholic Encyclopedia*. Retrieved from www.newadvent.org/cathen/07610b.htm

Potter, P. and A. G. Perry. (1993). *Fundamentals of Nursing* (third edition). Philadelphia: Mosby-Year Book.

Prather, J. (2009, June 18). "The game of King." Retrieved from thinkhebrew.wordpress.com/2009/06/18/the-game-of-the-king/

Salmas, S. (1995). *Depression Questions You Have … Answers You Need*. Allentown, Pa.: People's Medical Society.

Scofield, C. I. (1996). *The Scofield Reference Bible*. New York: Oxford Press.

Steinburg, A. (2003). *Encyclopedia of Jewish Medical Ethics*. Nanuet, N.Y.: Feldheim.

Stibbs, A. M. (1947). *The Meaning of the Word "Blood" in Scripture*. London: Tyndale Press.

"Daka" (def. 1). (n.d). In *Strong's Concordance Online*. Retrieved from www.bibletools.org/index.cfm/fuseaction/Lexicon.show/ID/H1792/daka.htm

"Dumanis" (def. 1) (n.d.). In *Strong's Concordance Online*. Retrieved from biblehub.com/greek/1411.htm

"Exousia" (def. 1) (n.d.). In *Strong's Concordance Online*. Retrieved from biblehub.com/greek/1849.htm

"Stubbornness" (def. 1). (2013). Retrieved from www.yourdictionary.com/stubbornness

Venes, D., ed. (2013). *Taber's Cyclopedic Medical Dictionary* (nonindexed version). Philadelphia: F. A. Davis.

Vine, W. E., M. F. Unger, and W. White. (1985). *Vine's Expository Dictionary of Biblical Words*. Nashville, Tenn.: Thomas Nelson.

Webster's New Universal Unabridged Dictionary. (1992). Avenel, New Jersey: Barnes & Noble.

"Saturation" (def. 1 and 2). (2010). *Webster's New World College Dictionary*. Retrieved from www.yourdictionary.com/saturate

Webster, N. (n.d.). In *American Dictionary of the English Language 1828 online*. Retrieved from webstersdictionary1828.com/

Corruption (def. 1). (1913). In *Webster's revised unabridged dictionary* (1913 + 1828). Retrieved from machaut.uchicago.edu/?action=searchandresource=Webster%27sandword=Corruptionandquicksearch=on

Wiese, B. (2006). *23 Minutes in Hell*. Lake Mary, Fla.: Charisma House.

Church of satan. (2014, January 28). Wikipedia. Retrieved from http://en.wikipedia.org/wiki/Church_of_Satan

Temple of set. (2014, January 20). Wikipedia. Retrieved from http://en.wikipedia.org/wiki/Temple_of_Set

"Your Amazing Wonderful Brain." (n.d.). Retrieved from www.projectcreation.org/kid_zone/articles/kid_zone_detail.php?PRKey=83

Ziegler, E. and M. Cranley. (1978). *Obstetric Nursing* (seventh edition). New York: Macmillan.

Printed in the United States
By Bookmasters